$\mathcal{L}$EADING

$\mathcal{T}$ODAY'S

$\mathcal{F}$UNERALS

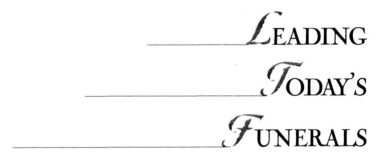

LEADING TODAY'S FUNERALS

A PASTORAL GUIDE FOR IMPROVING BEREAVEMENT MINISTRY

DAN S. LLOYD
FOREWORD BY RICHARD MAYHUE

Baker Books

A Division of Baker Book House Co
Grand Rapids, Michigan 49516

© 1997 by Dan S. Lloyd

Published by Baker Books
a division of Baker Book House Company
P.O. Box 6287, Grand Rapids, MI 49516-6287

Second printing, September 1998

Printed in the United States of America

Library of Congress Cataloging-in-Publication Data

Lloyd, Daniel Scott, 1958–
    Leading today's funerals: a pastoral guide for improving bereavement ministry / Daniel Scott Lloyd; foreword by Richard Mayhue.
       p. cm.
    Includes bibliographical references.
    ISBN 0-8010-9032-6 (pbk.)
    1. Funeral service. 2. Bereavement—Religious aspects—Christianity. 3. Church work with the bereaved. I. Title.
    BV199.F8L55 1997
    265'.85—dc21   97-1639

For information about academic books, resources for Christian leaders, and all new releases available from Baker Book House, visit our web site:

http://www.bakerbooks.com

Contents

$\mathcal{F}$OREWORD

$\mathcal{T}$wo things in life are inevitable—taxes and death. While tax resources abound, relevant helps to deal with death in the church and the community are few and far between. This hands-on manual will be a welcomed addition to the limited library available to pastors on carrying out this unavoidable aspect of their shepherding.

Pastor Dan Lloyd writes from a heart of compassion and a deep reservoir of experience in dealing with the myriad of issues relating to death. He has made a sizable contribution with this basic but thoughtful treatment of an eminently crucial pastoral responsibility.

Above all, the matter of one's eternal destiny is clearly treated from a thoroughly biblical perspective. Throughout, this volume affirms the truth that a personal relationship (or lack of one) with the Lord Jesus Christ in this life determines one's experience after death (Rom. 6:23).

Whether dealing with the death of a Christian, an unbeliever, someone previously unknown, or a member of the congregation, pastors will discover *Leading Today's Funerals* to be unusually helpful.

Richard L. Mayhue, Th.D.
Senior Vice President and Dean
The Master's Seminary
Sun Valley, California

$\mathcal{A}$CKNOWLEDGMENTS

I want to give thanks to those who helped make this book a reality. My greatest appreciation goes out to the many families I have ministered to over the years. Their patience with me in the midst of their loss has enabled me to learn how to care for hurting families. May these lessons be multiplied many times over as ministers who read this book care for other families in their times of loss.

I also want to thank members of the staff at Price-Helton Funeral Chapel in Auburn, Washington. Their willingness to allow me to work with families as an on-call minister provides me opportunities to develop my ministry skills. Working with Price-Helton is always a joy. It is a top-notch organization.

Without the support and prayers of my number one mother-in-law, Dr. Joan Franklin, this book could not have been written. As a writer herself, she patiently and persistently gave me the perspective and encouragement I needed to keep on writing. Joan also helped me with the huge task of editing my first manuscript.

Gratitude also goes to my friends in the ministry who read this manuscript and offered suggestions for improvement. Specifically, I would like to recognize Tim Crabtree of Tetelestai Christian Center (Torrance, California), Kris Kramer of Camano Chapel (Camano, Washington), Tim Klerekoper who is a King County (Washington) Police chaplain, Gary Klontz, president of Price-Helton Funeral Chapel (Auburn, Washington), and Orville Ward of SeaTac Bible Church (Federal Way, Washington).

I appreciate my friend and former pastor Dr. Richard Mayhue, dean and vice-president of The Master's Seminary (Sun Valley, California) for writing the foreword to this book and being a consistent example to me of what it means to be a man of God.

Finally, I would like to thank Paul Engle at Baker Book House for positive support throughout the long process of writing and editing.

INTRODUCTION

PREPARING FOR SIGNIFICANT MINISTRY

$\mathcal{B}$arbara's most dreaded nightmare has become a cruel reality. Death has stolen her child and shattered her identity as a mother. Everything about life now seems so unreal, like a blur that leaves her head and heart spinning. She replays the incredible events in her mind as she awaits an unwelcome pastoral call.

"Dead? Just the other day we were laughing and talking around the breakfast table. My only daughter arrived home from college and dreamed of a summer full of fun, beginning at the lake with old friends from high school.

"I was concerned that the party seemed to last so long. I hoped she was safe at a friend's home and that she would call to check in with me. But the hours continued on. I tried to convince myself that she would be all right.

"She had been drinking? How could that be? She knows better than that. And to be driving on such a dark and winding road! There must be some mistake. The police must have misidentified my girl. Someone borrowed her car. That's it. She loaned her vehicle to another blue-eyed blonde. Her wallet was in the car, and the officer just thought it was my daughter at the wheel.

"My baby would never drink and drive. She couldn't have hit that other car. She's a better driver than that. If she had known there was a young family in the other car she would have gone out of her way to avoid hitting them.

"How much longer am I going to be tormented by these thoughts? Why can't I just wake up from this bad dream and get on with my life? I want to hold my girl. I want to hear her laugh. I want to see the sparkle in her eye that warmed so many hearts and turned so many heads.

"Dead. What an ugly word. It's so . . . permanent. Now a stranger is coming over to talk about the funeral. Funeral. This can't be happening. I've never been to church and a minister is going to be in my house. I don't want him here. I want my daughter. What does this guy want from me? A confession? Does he think I'm responsible for all of this? He probably has it all figured out by now. Wait until he finds out I'm divorced. He'll pigeonhole me like all the others. 'You should have gone to church. You should have stayed married. You should have done this. You shouldn't have done that.' He probably thinks my 'sin' made an alcoholic out of my daughter. The doorbell. That's probably him now."

Your One Opportunity

You only get one chance to make a good first impression when called upon to help families manage significant loss. Your first few moments with them can lay a foundation for hope or alienate them from the One who is our hope. It is therefore important to prepare yourself for meaningful ministry as soon as you are contacted by the funeral home.

If you have been in the ministry very long, you know there is no such thing as routine crisis intervention. A family crisis is precisely what you face when called upon to help with a funeral. Rarely is a family ready for the death of a loved one. Even if there was notification of terminal illness or the threat of death, few people realistically anticipate their responses to that final farewell. The family's pain and confusion are intense.

Your purpose is to comfort and to guide. There may be many questions, expressed and repressed. You will not have all the answers. Your responsibility is to offer the care, compassion, and love of our Lord to people whose dreams have been freshly shattered. You can provide objective strength rarely seen even in the closest of friends if you know and fulfill your ministerial role as a helper.

When it comes to negotiating the consequential curves of death, families are not looking for a Grand Prix champion in a clerical collar. Instead, they appreciate a person who listens and takes interest—one who is warm, caring, honest, and real. Hurting families need a comforter who demonstrates the love and compassion of Christ while performing even the most painful tasks of ministry. Let the Holy Spirit care for them through you. Significant ministry does not happen automatically. Applying basic ministry skills can enhance your ability to share the love and compassion of Christ. You need to develop those skills, allowing the Lord to infuse them with spiritual power and produce life-changing effects among those you serve.

This book introduces you to skills that will enhance your funeral ministry. Applying its principles will also help you perform other pastoral duties with greater effectiveness.

Most pastors I talk with tell me that they received little or no training for funeral ministry. I received no specific training in Bible college or seminary for what has become a significant part of my pastoral ministry. Yet in my first ten years after seminary I performed more than one hundred fifty funerals. I have searched for reference works that can equip me to do better funerals. Most available resources are filled with sermons and poems. Not one funeral-related book in my library explains how to handle a prefuneral interview with a family, how to design a personalized service, or how to conduct a funeral service. I know of only one reference that describes how to follow up with a family after the funeral.

I have taught some workshops on how to lead funerals. Many participants encouraged me to expand my material and make it available in written form. In your hands is the result of my research and practical experience.

My prayer for those of you who read this book is that God will give you a fruitful ministry in assisting families who are working through the loss of a loved one.

CHAPTER 1

UNDERSTANDING THE PURPOSES OF A FUNERAL

*A*ttending a funeral is like visiting the dentist. We do not like it when another person pokes around inside our mouths with sharp metal objects. Nor do we enjoy gathering around a casket to pay our respects to the dead. Dentist visits are inevitable, however, if we want healthier teeth. And funerals can help us cope with loss.

People will go out of their way to have their teeth cleaned and repaired by a dentist who is well trained, highly skilled, and knows how to comfort anxious patients. My family, for the most part, enjoys visits with our dentist, Dr. Stephan, and his friendly staff. We drive more than twenty miles so he can work on our teeth. If you can learn to handle funerals the way my dentist cares for our teeth, people will leave your service the way patients leave his office, thinking, "That wasn't so bad after all."

Funerals are not supposed to be fun, but neither should they be torturous. When you understand the purpose of a funeral, you can set guidelines for yourself to make sure you lead a service that comforts those who are present.

Funerals Help Us Grieve

Grief is a normal response to loss. All of us need to meaningfully work through personal trauma or disappointment. Funerals can help us do that.

Culture shapes the way we react to the news of death. People living in Bible times often tore their clothes, wore sackcloth, or covered themselves in ashes (2 Sam. 3:31). They loudly wept and wailed as the mourners did in Mark 5:35–38. Families sometimes even hired professional mourners to grieve publicly for them (Jer. 9:17–18).

In some places of the world today, people still grieve in similar ways.

The Ayatollah Khomeini ruled as Iran's outspoken religious leader until his death in 1989. During his public funeral procession, nearly a million people gathered to remember their leader. The frenzied crowd roared and scrambled to touch his casket as it was lowered by helicopter toward the grave. Horror rippled through the masses when the pressing crowd upset the casket, spilling the body onto the ground. *Time* magazine reported that in the confusion of the crowd's mourning, 8 people were crushed to death. The report added that 440 people were hospitalized and 10,800 more were treated for injuries.

Westerners are far more subdued. We have learned to limit any public display of grief to our attendance at a funeral service, which is usually well planned and controlled. Such a tradition is neither inferior nor superior to those of other cultures. Funeral attendance is simply one of the more popular and acceptable expressions of grief we have adopted and affirmed over the years.

Funerals Help Us Express Sympathy

Individuals who experience loss feel lonely, confused, and sometimes abandoned. It is natural to want to display our sympathy to a family facing the pain of losing one of its members. Attending a funeral is a tangible way of expressing compassion and support to the hurting. Our presence also reaffirms our love for and commitment to those who have lost someone special. Death unalterably changes relationships, and it is comforting for the family to have friendships strengthened through the presence of friends at a funeral.

Funerals give us permission to let our defenses down and, perhaps for the first time, demonstrate feelings for those who are still alive. We give flowers, speak words of sympathy, and shed tears of sorrow. Family members and friends embrace, reaffirming present relationships while saying good-bye to one who has been lost. Family members who have been at odds with one another or who have had difficulty displaying affection sometimes begin to warm to one another as they gather around a casket to say farewell to a loved one.

Funerals Help Us Accept Loss

Grieving is the process of emotionally adjusting to loss. For many, reality takes on a surrealistic quality. Some call this the shock phase. I have heard hundreds of people say, "I can't believe it. This isn't happening. This is like a dream." Even years after someone's death, I have heard people say, "I still can't believe he's gone." Funerals force us to face the fact that death has taken a loved one from us.

Fred Rogers, of the children's television show *Mister Rogers' Neighborhood,* writes in his pamphlet *Talking with Young Children about Death,* "I've come to believe that anything human is mentionable, and anything mentionable can be manageable. It's not easy for any of us to accept that all living things, including ourselves and those we love, will die."

The sooner we can begin talking about the death of a loved one, the sooner we will be able to accept fully that loss without feelings of guilt or accusation. Funeral planning, even at the last moment for an unexpected death, causes people to talk about death and therefore deal with it more realistically.

Family members will sometimes remain silent and aloof when funeral preparations are being made. Yet at the service, words and feelings begin to come out. Often, it takes the presence of family, friends, and the minister around the casket to drive home the painful reality that a death has really occurred.

Funerals Help Us Remember Positive Times

Funerals are wonderful opportunities for remembering the positive highlights of a person's life. You can learn a lot about the depth of family relationships when preparing for a funeral. Close and loving families find it easier to remember and reflect upon positive things about the one who has died. They are more comfortable talking about the person's failures, and their shortcomings as a family.

Even when life has been hard on a family, positive memories remain to be remembered and shared at a funeral. Something nice can be said about even the wickedest person. I once heard about a lady who was known for her complimentary attitude. She never said anything negative about anyone. When asked what she thought of the devil, she said, "He's persistent."

Funerals Motivate Us to Make Memory Investments

Funerals challenge us to make "memory investments." You make a memory investment when you establish an annual event or tradition your family will cherish in the future. (For some wonderful ideas on how to build memories with your family, I recommend Gloria Gaither and Shirley Dobson's *Let's Make a Memory*.) Memory investments increase the quality of a family's life now and can reduce the pain of expressing love and appreciation for a loved one at the time of death. I encourage people attending funerals I conduct to continue the traditions that were of value to the one who has died. In this way the family can look forward to honoring its loved one and maintaining a sense of family stability.

When my mother's side of the family gathers for a special meal, someone inevitably will say in a deep, gravelly voice, "Nostrovia." My Ukrainian grandfather often would give that brief toast, which means "to your health," when he was still with us. He would prepare his famous beet and horseradish sauce for our Easter meal. Although we loved the flavor of his sauce, it is a tribute to Grandpa Kraynyk that no one has tried to recreate his special contribution to the annual Easter meal since he died.

Funerals Help Us Find Hope

Funerals are excellent occasions for giving hope to those who feel they have lost all hope. Biblically speaking, hope is the assurance or confidence that God will do what he has promised. Which of God's promises ought to be emphasized in a funeral? Certainly the forgiveness of sin, the promise of eternal life for all who trust Christ as Savior, and the assurance of God's presence and love are common themes.

When you talk about hope, be sure to clearly explain what God's promises are and how they are to be received. You need to pray about and discern which of his promises you will emphasize. I recommend those that specifically meet the needs or answer the questions of the family (or larger audience if appropriate). A good resource is *The Bible Promise Book*.

When the space shuttle *Challenger* exploded, killing its entire crew, the memorial service for Commander Dick Scobee was held in the church where I was a staff member.

Dick grew up in the town in which I live, and sometimes attended the church where I used to serve. His uncle, a local minister, led the service. He used 2 Corinthians 5 to bring hope and comfort to a nation shocked by another technological tragedy and the loss of seven lives. There was still some question if the bodies would ever be found. The minister used that uncertainty to bring us hope from God's Word. A tremendous opportunity for finding hope through the gospel of Jesus Christ was presented in a national tragedy.

Funerals Help Us Express Respect

When death strikes, it is not uncommon to hear people say, "I just wish there were something I could do for the family." Or "If I could only tell her again how much I appreciate her." In both instances, the speaker is really saying, "I would feel much better if I could tangibly express my love for this person right now."

Love desires to express itself in meaningful ways. Love does not die when a friend does, but it still seeks expression. Funerals provide an excellent opportunity for people to "pay their respects."

My son Stephen was devastated when our dog killed his parakeet. After regaining his composure, Stephen put the bird in a Ziploc bag. He gently placed it in a coin bank that looks like a safe and put it on top of the television (with the vault door open). For two days Petey lay in state while our family paid respects to the bird. Later, alone, Stephen buried the vault in a flower bed shared with our neighbors and placed a flat rock in the ground as a grave marker. His way of handling the loss reflects the way we customarily behave when we lose a friend or family member. The only difference between what he felt and the way we feel when humans die is the degree of loss. The important thing to Stephen was that he found a tangible and meaningful way to show his love for his pet.

Expressing respect for the dead is our way of affirming to ourselves, not the deceased, the depth of our love and the quality of our relationship. Still, acting on this need can have devastating effects on the family. Feelings sometimes tempt people to buy the most expensive casket, the largest floral spray, and the most scenic burial plot.

Does the corpse benefit from a softer casket mattress, a more colorful display of flowers, and a nice view at the cemetery? Of course not. These choices are for the benefit of the living, and such choices are understandable. But while it is not wrong to purchase a top-of-the-line casket, it is always wise to think through the reasons for choosing expensive items. Equating dollars with devotion is not always a balanced formula. Stewardship and affordability must be taken into consideration along with meaningful expressions of love when purchasing funeral services and products.

Funeral directors often will leave the room while a family selects a casket or other services for a loved one. This is done to avoid giving the impression that they are pressuring a family to purchase the more expensive items or services. Bereaved families are encouraged to bring a friend to assist in selecting options when funeral arrangements are made.

Funerals Help Us Prepare for Death

I often tell people that the only real guarantee in life is death. As ambassadors of Christ and ministers of reconciliation (2 Cor. 5:14–21), we have the obligation and privilege of helping others prepare for life after death.

Funerals are sobering experiences. The frailty of our existence becomes clearer at a funeral, especially when death takes a young person. Because this is true, funerals are the best opportunities I know of to prepare people for their own death.

With the exception of Enoch, Elijah, and Jesus, the grim reaper is statistically perfect in accomplishing his objective. The mystery for all of us is not *if* he will succeed but *when* he will knock on the door. This is not to sound fatalistic or ignorant of God's sovereignty. The Scriptures clearly state that our lives are planned by God even before conception (Judges 13:3–5; Ps. 139:13–16; Jer. 1:5), and that our days are numbered by him (Job 14:5). Yet, not one of us knows when the number is going to be called. Because we do not know what the future holds, we need to be ready for anything—especially eternity. I remind the people listening to me that no one knew one week ago we would be at this funeral remembering this person. I add that we have no guarantee we will not be back next week to pay respects at your funeral.

Though funerals are excellent evangelistic opportunities, they are not times to *push* evangelism or beat people over the head with the Bible.

One person told me about a funeral for a family member in which the minister said to the audience, "This person who died is in heaven and if you ever want to see her again you need to come up to this pulpit and get right with God." That is an abusive display of pulpit power and should never be the tactic we use in sharing the good news of Jesus Christ. Instead, we ought to be compassionate as we encourage the lost to come to Christ.

Funerals Do Not Help the Dead

People subscribe to a variety of erroneous thoughts about the role funerals play in aiding those who have died. A family once told me it wanted me to do a funeral service so I could be there when the spirit of its loved one ascended into heaven. I explained that at the moment of death Christians go to heaven (2 Cor. 5:8), but I would be happy to help the family remember and honor its loved one during the service.

Although denominational and cultural teachings vary, the Bible is consistent when it speaks of the afterlife, who gets into heaven, and how a person gets there. No effort made by humans or religious institutions has any effect on an individual's spiritual condition beyond the grave. Only by receiving the Lord Jesus Christ as Savior before death is anyone granted entrance into God's eternal kingdom. Jesus told Nicodemus in John 3:3, "Unless one is born again, he cannot see the kingdom of God." Hebrews 9:27 makes it clear that "it is appointed for men to die once and after this comes judgment."

I believe many ministers, in an effort to comfort grieving family and friends, want to make positive statements about an individual's spiritual condition. I co-officiated at a service with a minister from a denomination that does not believe in or teach the need for a personal relationship with Christ for salvation. The lifestyle of the person who died reflected his lack of spiritual values. Yet, the other minister assured the family that the man was with the Lord. What a tragedy to give that kind of false hope and imply that reckless spiritual living will be excused by God.

When it was my turn to speak, I admitted that we all knew this man had weaknesses along with strengths. I said Jesus Christ came to Earth because we are weak and helpless. I explained that Jesus took our sins to the cross so they could be removed by his blood as we place our faith, personally, in him alone for forgiveness and the assurance of eternal life. Nothing I said, however, benefited the one we were remembering. The only positive thing I could do was to tell his family and friends how to go to heaven when they die.

CHAPTER 2

PREPARING FOR THE SERVICE WITH THE FAMILY

*F*irst impressions are lasting. It is imperative that you meet with the family or friends to prepare for the funeral. How you conduct yourself at that meeting will set the tone for what happens at the church, funeral home, or graveside. You need to communicate compassion for the grieving and confidence in what you are doing.

One reason people dread funerals is that they fear losing their composure. If we fulfill the biblical admonition to be compassionate, caring, sensitive, and helpful (Col. 3:12–16), we can better prepare people for a funeral service. I have found the points below to be of great value when working with families before funerals.

Pray

If you are not in the habit of praying over your responsibilities and appointments, today is the day to start. More is accomplished when you pray first. Martin Luther once said,

"I have so much to do today that I must spend my first four hours in prayer."

Nobody prays enough, yet God honors those who do—even if they pray with a little bit of faith. Jesus told his disciples that faith the size of a mustard seed can move mountains (Matt. 17:20; 21:21). I have often wondered what residents of the Pacific Northwest would do if someone in the church put Mount Rainier into Puget Sound by faith. If a little faith can do that, why shouldn't you ask God to prepare the hearts of those with whom you are planning a funeral?

When I pray about the people I will meet with, I ask the Lord to help me represent him in a loving, compassionate way. That means I must put family members' needs first by listening well, using understandable terminology, not assuming they know everything that is going on, being patient when they don't know what to say, and remaining flexible about how our meeting and the service ought to be handled.

The Lord can comfort families through us not only when we meet with them but when we pray for them. If you do not have others who pray for you and your ministerial responsibilities, enlist them as soon as you can. The apostle Paul and other men greatly used by God constantly sought the prayer support of others. Colossians 4:2–3 says, "Devote yourselves to prayer, keeping alert in it with an attitude of thanksgiving; praying at the same time for us as well, that God may open up to us a door for the word, so that we may speak forth the mystery of Christ." Such support can help you clearly and powerfully speak for him.

If you are a pastor and you have not preached on the subject of intercessory prayer, you might consider challenging your congregation to pray for you. Your people are interested in the opportunities you have to mingle with and minister to those who do not know the Lord. Members of your church not only want you to challenge them to reach others for Christ, they want and need you to model evangelism. They can be participants in your ministry as they pray for you.

The Lord gave me a wonderful gift in my secretary, Barb, who helped me for seven years before she retired. She prays more faithfully than anyone I know. She and others in our church pray for me regularly, and their prayers work. It is a great comfort for me to know that when I go into a stranger's home or when I am performing a funeral service, others have been praying for me.

Practice SOLER

Gerard Egan, in *The Skilled Helper,* isolates five points of nonverbal communication which can be expressed in an acronym as SOLER. Here is what the acronym represents:

Squarely. Squarely face the person with whom you are speaking.

Open. Maintain an open posture when communicating.

Lean. Lean slightly toward the person with whom you are speaking.

Eye. Maintain eye contact while talking.

Relax. Try to remain relaxed and comfortable while communicating.

These guidelines can help you be aware of the impact of your nonverbal communication. You may feel awkward as you begin developing these skills. In time, they will become natural and greatly enhance all of your communications. Try using these techniques with SOLER when you visit with a family to prepare for a funeral service.

Squarely. After you are seated in the home, directly face each person with whom you are communicating. Turning toward whomever is talking at the time will communicate that both the speaker and what is being said are important to you.

Open. Maintain an open posture. You will probably be seated on a chair or sofa or around a table. Although you may be very comfortable with the people you are visiting, you may inadvertently send a different message. In our culture, crossed arms and legs can symbolize a closed attitude. Keep your hands on the table and both feet on the floor. This may sound a bit silly, but it is important. Try talking with your wife while your arms and legs are crossed. Then ask her to interpret your attitude in the conversation. She will make my point.

Lean. An occasional slight forward movement with the upper body "locks" your interest into the person who is talking. Leaning, especially when that person finds it difficult to communicate, shows you are listening and encourages the person to bring out what might be painful, uncomfortable, or even risky.

Eye. Eye contact also tells the other person you are interested and signals that you are truly listening. The most uncomfortable conversations I have are with people who will not look me in the eye.

I recently saw a friend in town. We talked for about three long minutes. Rarely did we make eye contact, although I tried desperately to do that. If he was not watching traffic as we talked, he was looking at my ear. While eye contact is vital, don't bore a hole through the other person's pupils. It is appropriate to break contact now and then so the other person won't feel as though you are invading his space.

Relax. If you are not comfortable, others will not be comfortable. The family will be disturbed by the death and may be wary of having a minister in the home. When you are nervous and tense, the situation can grow worse.

Follow a Plan

There are many practical things you can do to project calmness when you visit a family, but the best advice I can give you is to be prepared. Here are some ways to effectively guide a family while arranging a funeral service.

Take Notes

Use a notebook. You might want to prepare printed sheets on which to record critical facts. (See appendix A for a sample.) Be accurate but don't make the family wait for you to record every jot and tittle. Write down just enough to jog your memory. Note-taking assures the family that you are listening well and that you want accurate information for the service.

If you do not know the family, write down the names of the people you meet. I have found that families do not mind you recording the names of people with whom you are talking. They realize you are in a room full of strangers. List names in a logical sequence, such as in a diagram that represents the seating arrangement before you. When someone speaks, glance at your list and be ready to use the person's name when you reply.

The data you record will provide many benefits. Recently, a lady asked me if I would conduct her wedding. She called me because I had led a memorial service for her brother more than two years before. Checking my records I saw that I also held an informal service for the family a few months later when the remains were buried. I reviewed my notes just before that burial service and greeted each family member by name. When they commented on my tremendous memory, I told them I had reviewed my records. They appreciated not only the time I took to do that but my honesty in telling them why I knew each name.

Use the Deceased Person's Name

Write down the name of the person who died and use it often. Although you may not have known the deceased, family members will appreciate your personal reference to their loved one.

Be sure to confirm the pronunciation of the name before you visit the family. Representatives from the funeral home sometimes mispronounce names, so don't take their word for granted. When a name is unusual or difficult to pronounce, write symbols or other words that rhyme with the name. Families will appreciate your concern for accuracy.

Occasionally you will perform a service involving someone known by a nickname. Ask if the nickname would be appropriate to use. I led a funeral for a young girl whose brother's proper name is Fane. She referred to him as Faner. Trying to honor her love for him, I mentioned Faner during the service. Later, I learned the family did not appreciate that, because only his sister used that name. My reference to Faner took something away from its special meaning.

Ask Questions

Obtaining information from the family is easier when you guide the conversation through questions. Some families will bombard you with personal information, which always makes your job easier. Others may not know what kind of information you want, or may find it difficult to talk about their loved one. You need to draw out details through meaningful questions. Whenever possible, ask open-ended questions that cannot be answered with a yes or no. Develop questions designed to gather information about each of the following topics.

Personal Information

Record the birth date and, if the person was married (and the spouse is still living), the wedding anniversary date. The funeral home will tell you about the person's place of birth and date of death. You do not have to be too particular about these details when you prepare for the service with the family. Gathering personal information such as birth and anniversary dates is an expression of concern and care for the deceased as an individual.

You may want to send a note or card to a widow or widower on the next anniversary, or a brief letter to a parent on a child's next birthday. You can be sure those days will be especially difficult for the grieving family. A phone call or short visit a week, a month, and then a year after the service can provide tremendous comfort and love to those who grieve.

Many people have told me that because of the trauma and confusion surrounding a death, they did not remember who sent cards and flowers. If they receive a letter or card later, they know they have not been forgotten after the funeral. Go the extra mile. A brief expression of your continued care and Christ's love will mean much to the family.

I file basic information for each funeral. Into a computer database (alphabetized index cards also work) I load details about the deceased (name, birth date, wedding anniversary, date of death, cause of death, and age at the time of death), information about the family (names, addresses, phone numbers, and contact person), and notes about the service (date, name of funeral home and director, type of service, burial location, and additional comments).

In my filing cabinet I keep a copy of the clergy card, memorial card, notes taken when I met with the family, and notes I used during the service. Occasionally I will keep a newspaper obituary or news articles about the deceased.

Work/Career

We spend thirty percent of our adult lives on the job. Work is meaningful to us. If the person whose service you are preparing drew much significance from the workplace, you need to let the family talk about what work meant to that person. Learn about any promotions, awards, or commendations. Write down the names of close friends at work and have the family introduce you to them at the service.

Fellow employees are often excellent candidates for giving eulogies, because they spent so much time with the person who died, and knew the person so well. Some of the more meaningful eulogies I have heard came from those who used to work with the person who died. Ask if the family would like someone from work to say a few words in the service.

Personality/Lifestyle

Try to get family members to talk about what motivated their loved one. Was there a cause or organization to which the person was devoted, and why? What did the person do to support that cause or group? What was the person's philosophy of life? Was he outgoing or reserved? Did she have many friends, or did she stay to herself? Was there a phrase or saying the person often repeated? Was there a favorite joke? Did the person best express love through words or actions? Ask for examples. What was the highlight of the individual's life? Which life stories did she often tell? Was there ever a low point in life that he worked through and overcame? What was it like for this person growing up?

Ask about hobbies and recreational activities. They can reveal to others a part of life or memories cherished by the whole family.

I conducted a funeral for a friend who loved to search for bargains at the local swap meet. One of his prized finds was a hen that had been preserved by a taxidermist. Larry enjoyed showing the chicken to friends and laughing with them about his unusual treasure. When I met with the family to prepare for Larry's funeral, out came the chicken, and there was much laughter again. Even though I did not mention the hen in the service (and I probably should have), that bird did much to lighten the atmosphere while preparing for the funeral.

A woman whose service I performed had spent forty years tracing her family roots—to the year 536. Taking the time to look through a couple of her photo albums with her husband showed him that I had a personal interest in what had been meaningful to his wife and was meaningful to him. A little time goes a long way in helping everyone feel more comfortable when death strikes. You will also uncover a wealth of information that will help the funeral services be more personal and effective, even if you had not known the person.

Many questions can be asked if you take the time to think them through and write them down. I have found that families appreciate these kinds of questions. Such inquiries show that you want to take a personal interest in their loved one.

Occasionally a family will not say much about the deceased. Unfortunately, some families are not close enough to know the kind of information you want to gather. Others may think the details you seek are irrelevant and so they might not say much. Still others may be in too much emotional pain to talk. Be sensitive to the family's responses. If you think things are a bit too tense, back away, change the subject, and try to gather information later.

Encouraging family members to share memories may be the first time they have made any effort to speak positively about their loved one. More than once I have asked a family to talk with me about highlights of the individual's life and received blank stares in response. Many families have never talked about or demonstrated open appreciation for others in the family, even when family life was relatively good and positive. Attempting to verbalize appreciation when the pain of loss is so acute can almost be unbearable for many people.

I have performed services for parents who physically and emotionally abused their children. I have eulogized partners who have been unfaithful, others who were noted as the town drunk, and a son who died because of AIDS. I have held funerals for people who killed themselves or killed others. I remember watching one man in a wheelchair who had a difficult time looking into the casket to view his former wife. Those moments would have been so much easier for him, physically and emotionally, if she had not paralyzed him by shooting him in the back.

Here is an important lesson I have learned by doing these kinds of funerals. If you are not in the habit of regularly verbalizing your appreciation and love for individuals in your family, start doing that today. Your wife will appreciate knowing that you love her because of who she is, not just because of what she does. Your children will always remember hearing you say that you are thankful for them. Share how meaningful your memories are of times spent together with them. Let your children know what you were thinking and learning and experiencing when you were their age. It is a good idea to let family members know how you want to be remembered at your funeral and where they can find important information for handling arrangements at the time of your death. Your family will be deeply grateful for this kind of foresight.

Beliefs/Spiritual Background

I ask every family about spiritual beliefs, and no one has been offended, embarrassed, or uncomfortable talking with me about it. The family usually assumes the subject of religion will come up anyway, so go for it. I say something along these lines: Tell me about your husband's spiritual beliefs. Or I'll ask, Did your daughter ever talk with you about her faith? If she did, it's easy to ask, What did she say? If not, What do you think she believed?

These are nonthreatening questions because they do not require family members to express or defend their own theological convictions if they have any. This information will be important for personalizing your presentation of the gospel during the service, so be sure to ask about what the person believed.

If the family is comfortable in talking about spiritual things, this might be a good time to explore other family members' beliefs. You may want to ask, What has this death done to your own spiritual beliefs? If the deceased believed in God, try saying, Tell me about your own faith. How has it helped you in the last couple of days?

Don't pressure family members for a spiritual conversation or decision. If they are open to more information or want to make some sort of commitment, they will let you know. Allow the family to give you permission to explore this area. If the family has had bad experiences with pushy Christians and thinks you are pushing, it may have a difficult time hearing what you have to say in the home and at the funeral.

I believe the only reason a family would resent the subject of religion is if I tried to change or correct beliefs without an invitation to discuss spiritual matters in detail. Preparing for a funeral is not the place to confrontationally correct another person's theology.

In discussing spiritual matters, a family may want you to say or do something you know is biblically forbidden. One family wanted me to state that the spirit of its son was now residing over the motorcycle trails the family often rode. In the service, as I was preparing the audience to hear the gospel, I said something like, "The family expressed to me that they believe the spirit of their son is now residing over a town named Cle Elum where they often rode motorcycles. I can certainly see why that was a favorite location for the family. Cle Elum is a beautiful place. But God has a better place, a more beautiful place than Cle Elum, waiting for us in heaven when we die." At that point I shared with the family and the audience how to know for sure that each one of them could go to heaven. Though it is beneficial to accommodate families in every way possible, a minister of the gospel must never compromise major beliefs or an opportunity to clarify the truth.

Information about the Death

It may be difficult for you to talk about the manner of death, especially if you have not presided at many funerals. However, the family appreciates it when the minister shows enough interest to inquire about the death. This subject must be handled with discretion. The family may not know anything about the manner of death, or the details may be too grim to discuss. However, most families want to talk about even the most difficult means of dying. I have talked with parents about sudden infant death syndrome, with children about their mother's murder, and with a wife who witnessed her husband's suicide. Your control of the conversation and your level of comfort in talking about death will determine to a great degree the family's ability to discuss the manner of death.

You may want to say, "Tell me how your husband died," or ask, "Can we talk for a few moments about the manner in which your daughter died?" Use proper terminology, not euphemisms. For example, the terms death, dead, died, passed away, or passed on ought to be used rather than expired, graduated to glory, or worse yet, kicked the bucket or bought the farm. You may even need to be more direct and say, "Your mother was murdered (or killed by another person). Can we talk about that for a few moments?" Or "(Use his name) took his own life. Do you want to talk about that?"

Help people who may not know where to start with more open-ended questions or statements: "What have you been told about his death?" "How did she die?" "Tell me what you know about how he died." If another person was there at the time of death, say, "Tell me what happened when she died."

When you talk about the manner in which a person died, you are showing that death and the way people die is mentionable and manageable. You are showing personal and professional confidence in your willingness and ability to discuss an uncomfortable and often avoided subject. Families want and need to talk about the way people die. You can help them do that.

How to Be Remembered

Find out if the deceased ever talked about dying and personal wishes for a funeral. Many people do, and some even plan their own services.

An important question I always ask is, "If the person we are remembering at the service could say one more thing to us, what do you suppose it would be?" Families sometimes can answer this right away. Occasionally they need to reflect on their response. Once in a while, nothing comes to mind. In any case, don't force the issue. If you get some answers, you have a powerful resource at your disposal. In the service you can repeat what you have been told by the family. The words you say on behalf of the deceased carry a lot of significance. They are, in effect, the person's final words to family and friends.

Let People Grieve

No two people respond to loss in exactly the same way. Some are so familiar with it they can talk openly about what they think and feel. Some have been hit so hard and so often by death that they hide in silence, trying to avoid, again, the painful reality of losing someone. Still others are experiencing their first barrage of pain, grief, anger, and confusion, and are unsure what to do with all they are thinking and feeling.

It is never right to suggest that a person's response to loss is inappropriate. Remember, whatever behavior is exhibited is most likely that individual's best attempt at dealing with unfamiliar and unwanted circumstances and emotions.

People may say rude things or display unusual behavior as they learn to cope with their loss. At times we need to graciously allow these people to stumble through the mourning process. However, it might be necessary to show them more appropriate ways of managing grief. See ideas for doing this in chapter 8 on caring for the bereaved after the funeral.

Review the Service Format

Your final responsibility in meeting with the family is to discuss the details of the service. To say that you are conducting a funeral is too broad a statement. What do you mean by the word funeral? If it is a ceremony for remembering the dead, there are many ways to do that. Will the body be present? If so, will a burial ceremony follow a service in the funeral chapel or church? Families need to know the available options. A good funeral director will explain them and help the family make wise choices. As the leader for those services, you also need to be aware of the options.

Memorial Services

A memorial service is held when the body is not present. This is common when a person is buried far away from friends or family. A soldier might be buried overseas. A grandmother might be buried where she recently had moved, and a local service is offered so her friends can remember her together. As in the case of the space shuttle *Challenger,* memorial services may be held before bodies of accident victims are discovered.

On a couple of occasions I have led services for a family that, to avoid the pain of a funeral, had instructed the funeral home to bury the deceased with no one present. In time, however, the family realized it needed closure on the death and came together to formally lay the person to rest. The family continues to benefit from this decision because the burial place serves as a place of remembrance where members can visit and leave flowers.

Funeral Services

A funeral service is performed when the embalmed body or cremated remains are present. A burial service may or may not be included. Often, families are satisfied with a meeting at a funeral home or church without having to conclude the service at the grave.

The decision to have a memorial service is not hard to make. Circumstances of the death usually dictate the kind of service you will conduct. However, choosing whether to include a burial service can be tougher. Whenever possible, I encourage families to conclude the service at graveside. Although the kind of service you are to lead probably will have been decided before you meet with the family, the group may not know what should occur during the service. Many have never had to plan for such occasions.

You need to give the family a preview of what you intend to do for the service while being flexible about their personal ideas for the service. Let family members alter your plans if they want to. This is their time to remember their loved one. It should be personal and meaningful, bringing honor to the one who died.

I will never forget a memorial service for a young man who was killed in an automobile accident. As I entered the funeral home I could hear Pink Floyd's "Dark Side of the Moon" being played through the sound system. Looking at the group of people gathering for the service, I realized the music seemed to fit the audience well. The mood was becoming unusually bleak. I present the gospel at every service, but this time I felt the urge to make an exception. I sensed that the people would be defensive and that I should cater to the family's desire to keep the service nonreligious. As I asked the Lord for strength to minister to those who were assembling, I realized a spiritual battle was being waged for every person in the building. I could give the people what they wanted, or I could give the people what they needed. I read through Ephesians 6:10–20 again and made sure my spiritual armor was tightly secured.

When I stood at the pulpit, I saw a man from my church. He did not know the person who died, but he had taken time off from work to support and encourage me with his presence. He also sensed the spiritual conflict and prayed throughout the service that I would boldly make known the gospel.

Because through prayer I was strengthened to be bold, I told about Jesus Christ and the gift of eternal life he offers everyone. The Lord used Lance and me to change the atmosphere from one of gloom and despair to one of hope. As Christ's ambassadors, we can and must use every opportunity to tell others about the Reason for life, especially in the context of death.

A Few Words about Cemeteries

We have many prejudices about cemeteries. Many people are spooked by them. In childhood we saw monster movies and heard ghost stories that would have been bland without an event or two in a graveyard. People have been conditioned to feel negatively about cemeteries. Your confident presence and message of hope at a service near the grave can challenge some of those unfortunate biases.

A cemetery is not only where people are buried but where the living "visit" the dead. We go there to reflect, remember, and mourn, if necessary. Concluding a funeral at the graveside makes the cemetery and its surroundings seem more familiar and more comfortable when a family member returns to visit the grave.

It might be helpful at the funeral for a Christian to let others know that the word cemetery is derived from Greek words meaning "a place where people sleep." Cemeteries should remind us that death is not the end of life. They can reinforce visually the promise of God—to be absent from the body is to be present with the Lord (2 Cor. 5:8). What a wonderful witness to the power of Jesus Christ a cemetery can be. Rows of tombstones can remind us that many bodies of believers lie beneath the earth waiting to be reunited with their owners when Jesus Christ returns (1 Thess. 4:16).

CHAPTER 3

ORCHESTRATING
A MEANINGFUL SERVICE

ecause no two people are alike, no two funerals will be alike. Funerals, therefore, ought to be as distinctive as the one being remembered. Funerals are wonderful opportunities to make a lasting spiritual impression on those who are in attendance. Therefore, you ought to put just as much careful and sincere preparation into a funeral as you would a Sunday morning sermon.

You may not know every one whose funeral you perform, but you can orchestrate a meaningful service if you know how to organize and communicate the information given to you by family members and friends. Here are several things you need to know, with applications and illustrations that will help you present a service that is personal and meaningful.

Arrive Prepared

Ministry happens best when you are well prepared to serve. I like the story about the young pastor who thought he did not need to study before he preached his first sermon. He was confident that the Holy Spirit would speak to him when he stepped to the pulpit. He was right. The Holy Spirit said, "You're not prepared." Even those few who can preach from the hip need to prepare before they step down to the pulpit from having been in God's presence.

Plan to include four elements in the funeral: Scripture reading, the obituary, the eulogy, and prayer. In addition, taped or live music often is a part of the service. I usually insert music as a prelude, after my first prayer, or as a time for reflection at the end of the service. Don't be afraid to have two songs back-to-back if the family requests a lot of music.

The Four Major Elements

Scripture Reading

Reading from the Bible, especially the Psalms, can encourage those in need of comfort. Many of the Psalms were penned by those who suffered and then received comfort from the Lord. Saul asked David to comfort him with the songs he wrote (1 Sam. 16:23). I often read from Psalm 23, or a few verses from Psalms 90 and 91.

Many New Testament passages can remind the audience that a believer who died is in heaven enjoying the presence of the Lord. See John 14:1–3; 2 Corinthians 5:8; Philippians 1:21, 23; 3:20.

The Obituary

Our word obituary comes from the Latin word *obit,* which means departure. An obituary, therefore, is a written or verbal declaration of a person's death. It is customary to place an obituary in the local newspaper when a person dies. The funeral home can provide a copy for your records. If possible, review it before making preparations with the family.

Not every minister reads an obituary at funerals. I do, but prefer to keep the information brief, mentioning the pertinent facts: the person's name (check on pronunciation), date and place of birth, date and place of death, and names of survivors. Check with the family to confirm which survivors to mention and how to pronounce their names. If you do not incorporate an obituary in funeral services, you can weave such information into your comments.

The Eulogy

Eulogy is a transliteration of the Greek word that means "to bless." The eulogy is for saying good things about, or "blessing," the person who is being remembered. Try to have a friend or family member share personal memories, first-hand experiences, and anecdotes about the deceased. However, remember not everyone feels comfortable speaking in front of a crowd, especially at funerals.

If you are the one eulogizing the deceased and you did not know the person, mention that fact before you begin. Say that what you are about to relate is based on memories shared with you by family members. Explain that your purpose is not to tell family and friends anything new, but to review, with them, meaningful highlights of their relationship with this person.

To prepare a eulogy, review the notes you recorded while visiting the family. Look for themes or repeated ideas that surfaced. For example, I often comment on the person's life as a spouse, a parent, and a friend. Perhaps the individual had varied interests. Refer to the person's interests and hobbies. Try to illustrate with anecdotes.

I know a man who organizes his thoughts by speaking about the past (the individual's life history), the present (how to cope with the loss), and the future (how to comfort the family and prepare for one's own death). Find a system or pattern you are comfortable with, and use it. When you speak with confidence, your listeners can focus more intently through their pain on the words coming from your heart.

Some funeral homes offer the option of a video tribute. It incorporates pictures of the loved one with recorded nature scenes and music selected by the family. Video tributes are powerful, and the family can keep the tape. For information on video tributes, contact a funeral home.

Prayer

When you pray aloud in the presence of others, you are their representative or mediator before God. You must bring them to God as you speak with God. This means you must use easily understood language to which the average person can relate. If you use "Christianese" or King James English, there is a good chance people will feel alienated from something that is supposed to unify.

Try to keep the closing prayer brief. No one wants to sit through a lengthy funeral, and an extended closing prayer can make even a brief service feel long.

Know Your Audience

As with any other speaking opportunity, your first priority is to understand the needs of those you will address. Anticipate the questions and concerns of those who will be seated before you. I always assume two things about those who attend funerals: They do not want to be there, and they do not know the Lord. They may be very unlike the people in church on Sunday. Church attenders, for the most part, are there because they want to hear what is said and sung. People at a funeral, especially one for a family member, would rather be anywhere else.

Many who attend funerals rarely or never have gone to church. It is unwise to assume they understand spiritual matters the way churchgoers do. Avoid technical spiritual talk. State spiritual truths in everyday language without watering down the content of your message. Jesus did that, and he did it well.

A cassette recording of a memorial service reminds me of the importance of using common language. Here are excerpts from the minister's introduction to the Bible study he led during the service:

> The Word of God identifies death as being a promotion. "To live is Christ, to die is gain." Now those words, since we live in the cosmos, those words seem almost contradictory. Somebody dying, and it being gain. So we look up everything the Word of God has to say about this subject called death, we organize it, and we teach it.
>
> The doctrine of dying grace, point one: Dying grace is one of the six areas of God's grace, and refers to the physical death of a super grace believer. I know that the new people here will have no idea [about] some of the technical vocabulary we've adopted that refers to a spiritually mature believer.
>
> In dying grace, a spiritually mature believer is transferred from time into eternity under very special blessing. This was the case with Bob. Fully cognizant of the fact that he is dying, and that what he is facing is far, far better than living.
>
> Now, God is perfect sovereignty, perfect righteousness, justice, love, eternal life, omniscience, omnipotence, omnipresence, immutability, and veracity. God is one in essence, He is three in personality: Father, Son, and Holy Spirit.

This man kept on in that vein for another forty-five minutes. By his own admission, he developed a lot of the terminology to suit his own style of teaching. If you talk this way in Bible studies or while preaching, do not talk this way at a funeral. Use language people will understand. Make your comments relevant. Your purpose is to meet the people where they are and to serve them. You are there for them. They are not there for you.

Set the Tone

It is your responsibility to set the tone for the service. Many people believe a funeral is a morbid affair. But there is nothing morbid about a remembrance and celebration of life.

You can set a positive and caring mood before the service begins. If you do your job well in the family's home, grieving people will be more at ease as they arrive for the funeral.

You also set the tone as you pray during your preparation time. Ask the Lord to help you be sensitive, relevant, flexible, and accurate in all you say and do. Seek the Lord's help in preparing the order of service and choosing Scriptures that will speak to the hearts of those who are grieving. The Lord will honor your dependence upon his Spirit by granting you boldness and confidence in what you do for him.

Another way to set the tone for the service is to be there early enough to greet family members as they arrive. I attended a funeral at which the minister showed up three minutes before the service was scheduled to begin. Consequently, the funeral started ten minutes late. The family was nervous about his tardiness and was upset by his insensitivity in not apologizing for the inconvenience he caused. Promptness is important. Before the service is a good time to meet other family members and close friends. Your attentiveness will help them feel more comfortable with you and the service you lead.

It is sometimes awkward to meet strangers just before a funeral, especially if you do not know the one who died. In that case, try saying something like, "I didn't know (the person's name), but the family did a wonderful job in helping me to understand him. What can you tell me about him?" Ask people about their relationship or connection to the deceased. Make a simple comment like, "You must have loved her very much," or, "Thank you for being here today; I know the family appreciates your presence."

It is a good idea to ask if family members have any last-minute thoughts they want to give you. Often another thought has come to mind that is meaningful and should be shared. Family members occasionally have handed me poems and letters to read during the service. These have proven to be insightful and have helped personalize the service.

With the family, review the information on the clergy card provided by the funeral home. Although funeral directors are professionals, do not take their word when it comes to spelling, pronunciations, and vital statistics. The birth and death dates (including the year) listed on the clergy card for one of my funerals were identical. I did not notice that until I was reading the obituary during the service. Carefully reviewing and verifying that information would have spared me and the family embarrassment.

Continue to set the mood as the service begins. If you are escorting the casket down the aisle, slowly walk forward (not looking grief-stricken, shocked, or somber). Stop just past the front row of seats. Turn to face the casket and continue facing it until the funeral directors have put it in place. Then take your seat up front and wait for the prelude to conclude.

If the casket is already in place, walk into the chapel, find your seat, and listen to the prelude. Do not review your notes or read your Bible. Sit there and occasionally look at those in the audience, or the organist, or the balcony as you silently pray with your eyes open. Interact with people the same way at a burial service. You need to be with people if you are going to minister to them effectively. Then escort the casket as the funeral director indicates.

Be Accurate

Nothing will destroy your credibility as a minister and spoil a funeral service faster than misinformation. Accuracy is measured by the way you pronounce names and especially by what you say about the deceased.

Only rarely will you know the person who died better than members of the audience did. Don't try to fool them. I always tell an audience that I did not know the person who died when I am leading a service for a stranger. If I am not accurate concerning everything I say, or if I omit an obvious highlight in the individual's life, the audience will give me more room for error.

But sometimes accuracy hinders more than it helps. I once conducted a service for a young man who died of cancer the day before his first child was born. Adding to the misery of that occasion was a strong degree of jealousy between the man's wife and his sister. Because I wanted to be compassionate and balanced in the things I said, I made comments during the service based on information I had gathered from both women. I unknowingly made things worse by repeating key words and phrases that were flash points in the family feud. Fortunately, only family members knew what happened that day. They understood that I was not being malicious. They overlooked the offense because I was unfamiliar with the family situation.

Be Honest

People expect ministers to be honest. However, the temptation to say only complimentary things about the deceased must be overcome by everyone who performs a funeral. Should personal faults ever be mentioned at a funeral? This is certainly a tough question to answer. On several occasions a family has told me a loved one was no saint. I always agree, even if I did not know the individual. I have found that people would rather have me mention that a family member had problems than to try convincing people otherwise. We all know no one is perfect. Painting a picture of impeccability is not only dishonest, it erodes your credibility as God's spokesman before the public.

A brief comment is enough to acknowledge the flip side of an individual's character. I often put it something like this: "I have said a lot of nice things about this person today. Please do not misunderstand me and think that this man was perfect. There were times when he let you down, times when he hurt you, times when he failed. We have all failed. That is a part of life, a part of being human." This might be an appropriate time to present the gospel: "There is an answer to our imperfections: God's perfect Son, Jesus Christ."

Honesty also demands that you not supply nonbiblical or superficial answers to hard questions at the time of death. "Is my loved one in heaven? Why did she die? Couldn't God have stopped this from happening? Why would a God of love let my baby die?" These are important questions. If you have not been asked them yet, wait. They will come.

Be Relevant

Relevant means significant, appropriate, proper. Do those words characterize what you say in the pulpit? If your comments at a funeral are not marked by relevance, why should anyone listen to what you have to say? Your ministry will lack relevance if you have not considered, and put foremost in your mind, the needs of your listeners.

Relevancy takes time to develop. You cannot throw a few thoughts together and expect to say anything meaningful to a grieving audience. You cannot simply regurgitate a sermon from a funeral book and expect it to strike a healing chord in the hearts of mourners.

Here are samples of issues you might face in your funeral ministry. Be prepared to address them with the Word of God so you can provide solid answers to your listeners.

First, be sure to present the gospel message. Does the audience know the Lord? Do these people realize that Jesus conquered death? Do they know that Jesus is Life? In simple, clear terms help the people understand the significance of the theological statements you make. What better occasion is there than a funeral to share with people the provision of eternal life through Jesus Christ? His victory over death removes the fear and sting of death for the believer. That's eternal relevance.

Second, you need to make people aware that Jesus offers rest to the weary and heavy laden, and that his burden is light (Matt. 11:28–30). Those who grieve typically feel alone in their sorrow. This is normal for those who are suffering loss. Let your listeners know that Jesus cried when he learned that his friend Lazarus had died. Jesus did not weep because his emotions were weak but because his love was strong. Explain that Jesus understands pain because he experienced the same emotional suffering we experience. Tell them that Jesus promised to help bear their pain and give to all who believe in him the hope of a better life beyond this one (John 11:21–46). That's emotional relevance.

Be Brief

Nobody wants to attend a drawn-out funeral. Occasionally ministers forget that fact. I have found that a twenty-minute service adequately meets the needs of most families. If the family of the person who died did not attend church, the discomfort of sitting for a long time in a chapel may override what you and others have to say. The challenge is to keep the funeral short enough so the people do not feel as though things are dragging on unnecessarily, yet long enough to remember and honor the dead in a respectful manner.

Several teenagers from our town were killed in an automobile accident. The tragedy received much publicity and hundreds of teenagers attended the service. I am not sure why, but the minister chose to deliver a long sermon. After about thirty minutes of preaching, many of the teenagers began to walk out of the service. They were tired of hearing the minister ramble on about things that didn't matter to them. Their grief was overtaken by boredom. He seemed more wrapped up in what he was saying than how others were responding. He missed a wonderful opportunity to influence many young lives for Christ.

The most effective way to capture and retain the interest of your listeners is to make the service personal and meaningful through accurate, relevant, and brief verbal communication.

Present the Gospel

It is possible to present the claims of Jesus Christ even when the family requests a nonreligious service. I led a funeral recently for the wife of a new friend. The family had no church connections. Because the widower knew I was a minister, he asked if I would conduct the service. The only condition was that his daughter be given the freedom to write out the service. She had a bad experience with a "preacher" at her grandfather's funeral and was going to make sure the minister at her mother's funeral said and did only as she directed. Although the content provided for me was blatantly heretical, I decided to do the service because I knew the family needed the Lord.

After I welcomed those who were in attendance, I thanked the daughter for taking the time to write out the entire memorial service for me. I explained that because the daughter knew her mother better than anyone else, she could provide a unique personal touch. For the first time in my life, I read a manuscript from the pulpit. Not only did I want the daughter to know I was adhering to her wishes, I also wanted the people to get the impression this was coming from the daughter and not me.

Drawing from her theologically eclectic background, the daughter wrote, "The day of life is done, purified by the sunshine of a life well lived. I pass through the starlit portals of evening and bow to the approaching spirit. The candle honors the life and spirit of [her mother]; the incense honors the Deity and the flowers honor the spirit in each of us. As we reflect on life and death, we call to mind the following quotation: Beyond the power of sword and fire, beyond the power of water and wind, the Deity is everlasting, omnipresent, never changing, never moving, ever one." With that, a soloist sang "Ave Maria."

When I was done reading, I again thanked the daughter for taking the time and care to write out the words. I then folded the notes, placed them under my Bible, and began speaking directly to the audience. I said I wanted to share a few brief, personal comments before the service concluded. I began talking about Jesus Christ, and how a personal relationship with him could bring peace, healing, and comfort. My comments were gentle and brief. I did not want the daughter to have another disappointing experience at the funeral of a family member. Yet I was not going to let people leave without hearing about Jesus.

Later that week I received a note from the daughter thanking me for conducting the service. She did not appear to be upset or offended by my comments. I also received positive responses from Christians who had been present.

I wonder how many pastors would reject immediately such opportunities or simply lead a secular service. Turning down invitations to minister, especially when family members specifically request your services, may alienate them from Christ.

CHAPTER 4

WORKING WITH A FUNERAL HOME

My first two years of ministry after seminary were eye-openers for me. Although my experience in church staff work during Bible college and seminary was positive, my time with the next church I served was quite different. It did not take me long as associate pastor at the second place to realize I needed out. Shortly after I decided to resign from that ministry, I happened to see a local funeral director. He told me of the funeral home's need for someone who could assist families who had no church or pastoral contacts. We talked for a few moments about the possibility of me being an on-call pastor to the community. The prospect of reaching out to others in this way excited me. We agreed that I would be available whenever someone needed a pastor.

In the next five years I performed approximately one hundred twenty-five funerals. All but four or five were for people who had little or no spiritual background. In those years I learned many things about working with a funeral home. Whether you conduct only one funeral or hundreds, knowing how to work with a funeral home will benefit your funeral ministry.

Clear Communication Is a Must

Funeral directors and their staff are highly trained professionals who have developed efficient systems for doing their work. Listen to what they say. They will give you as much information as possible. I have found them flexible and willing to work with you in providing compassionate assistance to families.

Funeral home staff members are present to make your ministry the best it can be. You should try to do the same for them. The key to a mutually supportive ministry relationship is trust that is established and strengthened through clear communication. You and the funeral staff need to discuss and understand many issues.

Ministry associates need to know what to expect from each other in their cooperative efforts. Expectations need to be clarified so everyone can understand each one's role.

What do you need or want from a funeral home so you can offer your best help to hurting families? If you have never led a funeral before, or if you are relatively inexperienced at it, tell the director. He or she will be happy to help you develop confidence in leading services. It is also a good idea to talk with a pastor experienced in conducting funerals. The director can refer you to ministers whose funerals are excellent.

Set a High Performance Standard

Funeral homes often rely on the clergy to lead the public services. Naturally, funeral homes want the most compassionate and relevant communicators behind their podiums. The level of skill employed by a minister leaves a strong impression on the public about the quality and competency of the funeral home—especially if the service is in the home's chapel. There is no logical connection between the performance of a pastor and the competency of the funeral staff, yet people often make this kind of association.

Make an appointment with the funeral director in your town and talk about standards of performance. If you have already led funerals together, find out what you are doing that works well. Ask where you can strengthen your skills. What does the director believe you can do to be of greater assistance to the community at large? Discuss preservice preparation and postservice care.

Ask the funeral director if he is looking for an on-call pastor, and what he would like from someone who is available to those who have no church background or contact. Your interest in conducting a funeral with excellence and compassion might open doors to a new ministry in your community.

Once you establish standards of performance, abide by them. That's easier said than done, so review your performance after a funeral. Did you do what the funeral director said was needed to help this family? Ask the funeral director how you can provide a better service next time.

Clergy Cards

The funeral home will provide you with a clergy card with basic information about the deceased, such as name, date and place of birth, date and place of death, survivors, and a brief obituary. Use the card during the service and keep it for your own records. Check with a family member to make sure you understand proper pronunciations of all names. Do not take the funeral director's word for granted.

Order of Service

The funeral director and family will discuss elements of the service, but ultimately you decide how the service will be put together. After you have met with the family to prepare for the funeral and made your decisions about the service, make copies of a basic schedule for the funeral staff. Include copies for anyone who will participate, such as singers, instrumentalists, or other speakers.

If you use a computer or word processor, run the order of service through a spelling checker. If you type or write your information by hand, double check your spelling and punctuation. Careless writing, even if you produce a simple outline, will cast a bad light on your level of competence. Always strive for excellence.

Taping Services

Funeral homes sometimes offer families audiotapes or videotapes of the service. Often these are reviewed by those who attended the service as a continuation of the grieving and healing process. Sometimes tapes are sent to those who could not attend the funeral.

Because musical copyright laws are so strict, some funeral homes will not tape services that include music. Audiotaping or videotaping a copyrighted song without permission from the copyright holder is illegal. If a family wants a tape of a service, it is best to have the video camera or tape recorder pause while a song is performed. Don't simply brush off the responsibility of abiding by copyright laws because you do not own the camera or tape recorder. For information about copyright laws, contact a copyright attorney. For information on conditions under which your ministry may be licensed to duplicate or print copyrighted music, contact Christian Copyright Licensing International

(CCLI) by phone at (800)-234-2446 or by mail at 17201 N.E. Sacramento, Portland, OR 97230.

Honoraria

Because you are a professional, families expect to pay you for your services, and they should. Accept the honorarium gracefully. An exception might be when you perform a service for church members or members of your own family. Although I have conducted services for relatives, I do not recommend leading a funeral for someone close (spouse, child, parent, or sibling). You need to grieve at these kinds of funerals like any other person who has lost a close family member. Let someone else take charge when your loss is acute.

Two questions often arise over the issue of payment: How much and in what form should a minister be paid? Typically, a funeral director will answer both questions for families while discussing funeral costs and payments. Amounts are suggested, but the final sum is determined by the family. There are times when I have not been paid for my help and others when I have been paid several hundred dollars.

In the town where I live, the ministerium brought recommendations for payment amounts to funeral homes in the area. Yours might want to do the same. It is a good idea to invite one or two funeral directors to address a group of pastors in your area to discuss funeral-related issues. Arrange a tour of funeral homes. Ask directors to explain their procedures from the time they are notified of a death to any follow-up provided after the funeral.

Checklist

I have a friend who is a commercial airline pilot. Every time he enters the cockpit he goes through a series of preflight checklists. Although he has been flying for years and probably can recite the checklists from memory, he is still required to go through the routine.

A funeral checklist can help you ensure nothing is over-looked in your preparation and follow-up while working with families. A sample checklist is included in appendix B.

CHAPTER 5

HANDLING THE FUNERAL
FOR A NON-CHRISTIAN

*W*ithout a doubt, the most difficult service you will conduct will be for a non-Christian. Because God's Word is so clear, you and I know that the person who dies without Christ will spend eternity in the lake of fire (Rev. 21:8). Before being cast into that place, that person awaits final judgment in Hades, a place of fiery torment (Luke 16:22–24; Rev. 20:13–14). Two principles have helped me through scores of heartbreaking scenarios at funerals. One relates to the way I have learned to think about dead people in hell. The other deals with how to communicate with many non-Christians who are essentially obligated to attend funerals. I address these sensitive family issues by telling the positive side of the truth.

How to Talk about a Non-Christian

Unless you are sure the person being remembered is a believer in Jesus, it is wise to avoid saying whether the individual is in heaven or in hell. Although evidence may be abundant that the person who died lived a pagan lifestyle, God specializes in mercy and grace. Through those means, God offers a variety of ways every person can respond to him before being ushered into eternity (Rom. 1:18–20; 2:1). Many call upon the Lord on their deathbeds. I believe the Savior is just as pleased to rescue a penitent individual one minute before death as he is to redeem a child.

I tell the people at a funeral two things: God gave the deceased a chance to respond to him before death, and God is giving everyone a chance to respond to him right now. I note that God makes himself known to mankind in several ways, and for one reason: He wants us to know him through his Son Jesus. When we do find the Lord, heaven is ours also. Regardless of a person's spiritual beliefs, everyone is accountable to God for eternity.

God reveals himself to mankind through creation: "The heavens are telling of the glory of God; and their expanse is declaring the work of His hands" (Ps. 19:1–2). Acts 14:17 reveals, "He did not leave Himself without witness, in that He did good and gave you rains from heaven and fruitful seasons, satisfying your hearts with food and gladness." Finally, the apostle Paul made a very clear point when he wrote, "That which is known about God is evident within them; for God made it evident to them. For since the creation of the world His invisible attributes, His eternal power and divine nature, have been clearly seen, being understood through what has been made, so that they are without excuse" (Rom. 1:19–20).

God also reveals himself (and his law) through our conscience. "For when the Gentiles who do not have the Law do instinctively the things of the Law, these, not having the Law, are a law to themselves, in that they show the work of the Law written in their hearts, their conscience bearing witness, and their thoughts alternately accusing or else defending them" (Rom. 2:14–15).

God reveals himself, as well, through Christ Jesus, his Son. John wrote in his Gospel, "No man has seen God at any time; the only begotten God, who is in the bosom of the Father, He has explained [or revealed, literally exegeted] Him" (John 1:18). Jesus said, "If you had known Me, you would have known My Father also; from now on you know Him, and have seen Him. He who has seen Me has seen the Father" (John 14:7, 9). In his prayer before his arrest and crucifixion, Jesus declared, "I glorified [revealed] Thee on the earth, having accomplished the work which Thou hast given Me to do" (John 17:4).

Finally, God reveals himself through the canon of Scripture. Consider 1 Thessalonians 2:13: "We also constantly thank God that when you received from us the word of God's message, you accepted it not as the word of men, but for what it really is, the word of God, which also performs its work in you who believe."

Because God makes himself known in many ways, Paul concludes in Romans 1:20 that no one is without excuse before God. Every one of us will have to give a personal account to God when we leave this life.

Those attending a funeral for a non-Christian need to hear that their friend or family member was given a chance to know God and respond to him. They also need to realize that the person has answered to God for either rejecting or receiving him.

Regardless of the individual's eternal condition, there are at least two more things we know to be true that should also be communicated.

Every Person Who Has Died Knows the Truth about Jesus

First, the person who is dead now knows the truth about Jesus Christ, heaven, and hell. The one being remembered is no longer living in a physical world restricted by time or space. He is living in the spiritual world. That person has seen the Savior and understands that from which he can save us and to what he can save us. Like the rich man in Luke 16, the one who has died wants his family and friends to make the right spiritual choices before death. Let your listeners know that if the deceased could say one more thing to each of them, it would be to urge them to be ready for their own death by receiving Jesus Christ as Savior without delay.

Every Person Who Has Died Has Been Judged by Jesus

The other fact that should be communicated at a funeral for a non-Christian is that the person who died has been fairly judged by a God who is just. Hebrews 9:27 says, "It is appointed for men to die once and after this comes judgment." The deceased received what was due him. God did not tip the scales to rule for or against the person. An individual who responded appropriately to God's self-revelation is in heaven. One who did not, isn't.

There is nothing we can do to alter the departed one's spiritual condition. Faith in God is a personal venture, a relationship with the Creator through Jesus Christ. God's Son said, "I am the way, and the truth, and the life; no one comes to the Father but through Me" (John 14:6). Because a person chooses before death where to spend eternity, carefully give attention to the next matter.

What to Say to Those Who Attend

God doesn't want anyone to go to hell. "The Lord is not slow about His promise, as some count slowness, but is patient toward you, not wishing for any to perish but for all to come to repentance" (2 Peter 3:9).

Perhaps the reason those in the audience knew the non-Christian person who died is because they were led into his life so they would one day attend his funeral and hear the gospel. When focusing on the true needs of an audience, I emphasize two things: the uncertainty of life, and the certainty of heaven. Let's look at each one in detail.

The Uncertainty of Life

None of us knows enough about God's plans to say when our life will end. About the only thing we know for sure is that we shall all die (except for those few fortunate ones who will be raptured). Every person listening to a funeral message at the church, chapel, or graveside had a schedule interrupted by this death. The ultimate schedule interruption is one's own death. If the group you are addressing is anything like the population at large, most attenders are not ready to die. It is your responsibility to let them know how to be ready.

Funerals are wonderful opportunities for evangelism, but they ought not to be used to pressure or manipulate people into making a spiritual decision. Playing on the emotions of people is not fair. While we ought to use the opportunity to share the gospel, we need to let people respond to the Holy Spirit's prompting rather than our pressure or their emotions. Foxhole conversions are man's efforts to strike a deal with God. A typical grief-induced bargain with God is, "I'll do what you want if you do what I want." Often, what grieving people want is their loved one back or their pain to go away. God rarely makes such arrangements with hurting people. It has been a long time since anyone has risen from the dead.

On the other hand, the Lord can use funerals to plant the gospel seed in minds and hearts. God is creative, and he uses many things, even funerals, to bring people to himself. I have seen many people come to Christ at the time of a funeral. Those are wonderful experiences. Death is obviously on the minds of people then. They are thinking about their own mortality and asking questions about eternity. Some *want* to prepare for the future. Others have never stepped foot in a church or chapel and will hear the good news of the gospel for the first time. Perhaps a funeral will be God's way of drawing them to him.

The Certainty of Heaven

Emphasize the certainty of heaven. So many things on Earth go haywire. Plans fail, and people fail, but Jesus never fails. He promised to provide an eternal home for all who come to the Father through him (John 14:1–6). Don't just tell people how to get to heaven, tell them what it is like. Reflect upon Revelation 21:1–5 and Revelation 22:1–5. Try to incorporate these passages into your funeral presentation.

I recently conducted a funeral service for the mother of an elder in our church. She was a godly woman who loved the Lord. As I read at her graveside about the beauty of heaven recorded in Revelation, I was so filled with anticipation of being there myself I could hardly continue reading. Visualizing the wonder of our future home filled me with emotion and joy. There was no room for grief. Believers who attended were filled with joy as we celebrated the fact that Bertie was in the presence of our Lord and her loved ones.

Even in a service for a non-Christian you can emphasize heaven. While hell is a real place, and many will spend eternity there, it should not be the central theme to your words at a funeral. Instead, tell people how to go to heaven.

I share the gospel by stating that heaven and hell are facts. Even logic verifies the concept that eternity is a reality. How can time stop? If time goes on forever, what are people going to do once they die? To answer that troubling question various religious groups teach reincarnation (the ultimate recycling program) or annihilationism (we become nothing when we are gone). One emphasizes fatalism, the other futility. What sense does either make?

A funeral is not the place to argue eschatological differences. It is a place for you as a representative of Jesus Christ to declare the truth. An individual's response to the Savior will determine where that person will spend eternity. Talk about the Savior.

You may ask this question: "If you died today and you met God at heaven's gate, and he asked you, 'Why should I let you into heaven?' what would you say?" Give them a moment to think about their answer. Then ask, "If there is any other way to get to heaven than through Jesus, why did he have to die on the cross? If God is willing to accept your efforts to get into heaven, why was his Son crucified?" Stress that entrance into heaven is gained through personal faith in Jesus Christ.

Jesus made exclusive claims about himself and heaven while on earth. One is found in John 11:25–26: "I am the resurrection and the life; he who believes in Me shall live even if he dies, and everyone who lives and believes in Me shall never die." What a statement. When you believe in Jesus and live (physically), you will never die (spiritually). When you die (physically) after having believed in him, you will always live (spiritually). Who else but Jesus could do something like that for us? Those who believe in Jesus before they die go to heaven. Those who reject him are on their own.

CHAPTER 6

PRESENTING THE GOSPEL

I have never led a funeral without sharing the gospel. Whether the service was for a pagan or a saint, every audience I have addressed has heard how to go to heaven. We have an obligation to "preach the gospel to all creation" (Mark 16:15). We are to "be ready in season and out of season" to preach the Word of God (2 Tim. 4:2). What better "season" to share the good news about eternity with Christ than during a funeral?

Many families have asked me not to say anything religious at the service, and I assure them that I will not. Instead, I stay away from religious sounding words like saved and gospel during a service for a non-Christian. Even when we are remembering a believer, I make an effort to define such terms if I use them. It is easy to confuse and alienate those who are unable to decipher our religious code words. Spiritual terminology, however, is appropriate if your listeners understand its meaning.

Defining the Gospel

I will never forget a luncheon at which the speaker was a well-known pastor, radio personality, and author. Several of his books reflect his perspective on debates over the implications of believing the gospel. During a question and answer time, someone in the audience asked our guest, "What must a person believe to be saved?" His answer surprised me. After gathering his thoughts, he rambled off several things, such as the virgin birth, the deity of Christ, and the trinity. His answer was not accurate. I am not convinced an unbeliever can comprehend the theological concepts he mentioned. Even those who have known the Lord for many years may not have a solid grasp on such complex doctrines.

The Bible clearly states what a person must believe to be saved—the death, burial, and resurrection of Jesus. "Now I make known to you brethren, *the gospel* which I preached to you, which also you received, in which also you stand, by which also you are *saved*, if you hold fast the word which I preached to you, unless you believed in vain. For I delivered to you as of first importance what I also received, that *Christ died for our sins* according to the Scriptures, and that He was *buried*, and that He was *raised* on the third day according to the Scriptures" (1 Cor. 15:1–4, italics added).

Thus the Scriptures give us an objective way to evaluate the accuracy of the message we preach. We have a standard by which evangelistic materials can be measured. While working on an assignment for a class in Bible college, I discovered that most gospel tracts do not contain the gospel. The gospel is the death, burial, and resurrection of Jesus Christ. If you use tracts in personal evangelism, review their contents to see if they contain the gospel as outlined in 1 Corinthians 15:1–4.

Transition to the Gospel

It is important to make a smooth transition into a gospel presentation. Transitions can vary according to the circumstances. Try to establish a bridge from one point to the next, and make the presentation of the gospel a natural outgrowth of what you are saying.

My most common technique is to build on what I have learned about the person who died. Remember this key question—"If your loved one could say one more thing to those of us at the service, what do you suppose it would be?" The answer can come in handy here. When relaying those thoughts during the service, I am preparing the people to hear the gospel. I might say something like this: "I met with Sarah's family a few days ago to prepare for our service today. While I was with them, I asked a very important question." At this point, I would repeat the question and what the family thought Sarah's final comment might be.

The transition into a gospel presentation can come in one of two ways. If the person who died is a Christian, I would say, "There is one more thing Sarah wants you to know. Many of you already know that she believed in God. She talked with some of you about her faith in Jesus Christ. Others of you knew of her faith simply by observing her behavior. What Sarah wants you to know is that you need to be ready to meet God at the time of your death. Sarah was. Sarah has seen God and has accounted to him for her life. More than ever, Sarah knows the truth about the afterlife. More than ever, Sarah wants you to be ready for eternity. Let me tell you what Sarah believed, and how she prepared for eternity."

In the case of a non-believer, I would present the same information about the gospel, but the challenge here is greater because I am encouraging listeners to make a commitment to Someone the deceased may have rejected.

After repeating what I learned about Sarah from her family, I typically say, "There is one more thing I believe Sarah would want you to hear today. Let me preface that statement with these comments. Sarah *as a person* is not dead. Her body has stopped functioning, but she is still very much alive in the spiritual world. She is therefore no longer limited by time and space. The Bible teaches that the first thing Sarah did when she entered that dimension was to give an account of her life to God—an exit interview, if you will. I do not know what happened at that meeting. None of us knows. But Sarah knows and God knows. Because of that meeting, there are some things Sarah would want you to know before you give your answer to God for the way you lived." Then I begin the gospel presentation.

Notice that I did not say where I think Sarah might be. I can't make that kind of statement. I don't know where she is. I believe, however, that wherever she is, she wants her friends and family to hear the gospel (Luke 16:27–28).

A more generic approach can be used by commenting on the reasons we celebrate holidays. For example: "Easter is just around the corner. Although we enjoy watching children hunt for eggs and receive gifts in their baskets on Sunday morning, our hearts tell us that Easter is more than the celebration of spring, fluffy chicks, and the Easter bunny. It is not a celebration of *new* life, but more importantly the source of *true* life—Jesus Christ. Easter is the celebration of the resurrection of Jesus Christ from the dead. Have you thought much about why Jesus died on the cross? His death and resurrection paved the way for you and me to spend eternity in heaven with him." Now is the time to lay out the facts of the gospel.

Another transition is to refer to the cross hanging on the wall of the funeral chapel: "We've been here for twenty minutes or so, and you have listened to a lot of words. You have also noticed the surroundings. The flowers are beautiful. They are appreciated expressions of love. The music has been lovely. It has soothed our hearts and spirits. The seats are comfortable. They help us endure an uncomfortable purpose for our meeting today. There is a cross on the wall. It is a reminder of hope. The cross is more than a fashion statement to be worn around the neck. It is more than a religious symbol distinguishing Christians from others. The cross is God's reminder to you and me of his great love for us. The cross is the place where God's Son, Jesus, gave his physical life so you and I could find spiritual life through him."

Proclaiming the Gospel

I am not a big fan of canned evangelistic presentations, although I do appreciate the purposes they serve. For people who are learning to share their faith, memorized presentations are a great teaching tool. If he or she understands what has been memorized, the novice evangelist will gain confidence in sharing the gospel. Memorized presentations also assure trainers that the same message will be shared by all those they are equipping to evangelize. My concern is the implied message that evangelism is scary—you can't effectively do it unless you know this material verbatim.

Any memorized presentation should be seen as only a tool. I prefer to emphasize concepts, freeing the speaker to communicate in a more natural way. I use the acrostic FACT in training people to share their faith. In a nutshell, it represents these four facts:

Free gift (Eternal life in heaven is a free gift; Rom. 6:23b).
All have sinned (Rom. 3:23).
Christ died for your sins (1 Cor. 15:3).
Trust Christ for forgiveness (Rom. 10:9–10).

Free Gift

There are four things people need to know before they can go to heaven. First, God wants people to go to heaven. The Bible says eternal life is a free gift from God. Nobody earns the way into heaven. Everyone there arrived by the grace of God through faith in Jesus. That's the good news. Now here's the bad news.

All Have Sinned

Not everybody gets into heaven, and for good reason. Simply stated, sin blocks the way. Sin is not believing in or obeying God. The Bible says every one of us has done something wrong, and God is going to hold us accountable for our actions and attitudes. For us sinners, that's bad news. However, there is more good news.

Christ Died

The Bible says that Jesus died on the cross to forgive our sin. If sin can keep us out of heaven, the only way we can get there is by having our sins forgiven. The only way our sins can be forgiven is through Jesus, who died on the cross to forgive our sins. If sin could have been forgiven any other way, the crucifixion would have been a waste of time. Christ died for our sins, was buried, and rose again according to the Scriptures. That's really good news.

Trust Christ

If we want to go to heaven, we have to act on our belief in what Jesus did at the cross. We have to trust Christ. The way we trust Christ is by admitting that we are helpless apart from him. Without obedient faith in Jesus, we are all destined to spend eternity without him. We admit our need for Christ by confessing that it was our sin that put him on the cross. Trusting Christ means accepting the responsibility for sin, and by faith receiving the forgiveness of sins he offers.

The best way I know to express faith in Christ is to pray a prayer of faith. The prayer is simple, yet very important. It is an example of what it means to believe in Jesus. For those who want to go to heaven but know that sin is keeping them out, this prayer of repentance and faith is a good thing to express.

"Dear Lord, I want to go to heaven. I know I can't get to heaven because my sins are blocking the way. I also know that Jesus died on the cross to forgive all my sins. I take personal responsibility for my sins by admitting them to you. Because I know that my sins put Jesus on the cross, and on the cross he made forgiveness possible, I am now asking you to forgive my sins. I am asking you to allow me to enter heaven because of my faith in Jesus. I am trusting Christ to be my Savior by turning my life over to you. Thank you for forgiving me. Help me grow in my relationship with you. In Jesus' name, amen."

I have never had anyone object to this kind of gospel presentation. Even when families have asked me to keep the service nonreligious, they have welcomed the unpressured presentation I give. Many have positively commented on my statements about faith and going to heaven. One receptionist at a funeral home told me she makes a point to listen in on my services because she wants to know more about faith in Jesus. Your faithfulness in proclaiming the gospel can have an impact even on those who are not a part of the primary listening audience.

DIFFICULT FUNERAL SERVICES

*T*he most challenging ministry task I have ever faced was conducting the funeral for a dear friend. I saw John and his family come to Christ and grow in their new faith as they attended a Sunday school class I taught for new Christians.

As the years passed, God took a strong hold on John's life and used him as a powerful and effective witness to his family, neighbors, and coworkers. We prayed for and helped other members of John's family receive Christ. John often talked with me about his deepening love for his wife and two daughters, his growing burden for his fellow longshoremen, and the spiritual joy that was his.

In the spring of 1986, John called, as he often did, to fill me in on the latest events in his life. He was experiencing a personal revival, he said, and had ample opportunities to tell of his faith among his coworkers. Two weeks later, John's brother-in-law called with tragic news. John had been killed at work. A crane lock securing a metal support beam that had hoisted a yacht from a cargo ship broke, and tons of plummeting steel took John's life.

The pain of losing that dear brother nearly prevented me from speaking during his funeral service. I thought I had everything under control until I mentioned John's wife, now a widow, and his two precious girls, now fatherless. The tears that flooded my eyes and the emotion that choked my throat made it difficult to proceed.

I had to remind myself that I was not standing at the pulpit for myself—nor was I there alone. My purpose was to reveal the source of life to those who had gathered because of John's death. I could not have done what I did without the assistance of the Spirit of God within me. Jesus said he would send the Spirit to empower us to be witnesses for him (Acts 1:8). But that does not necessarily mean it's effortless.

I could not give John back to his family and friends. But I could offer hope, comfort, and assurance through Jesus Christ—once I realized that my life and my ministry are devoted to others and not myself. That perspective was the channel through which the Holy Spirit enabled me to care for those who needed strength through me in their time of need. I believe the Spirit of God desires to use every believer as a point of light in a darkened world, filling and empowering each of us to do the seemingly impossible.

No funeral is easy. Some are more challenging than others. This chapter gives insight on how to handle the tougher ones.

The Death of a Young Person

During my first trip to Israel, I visited the Holocaust Museum in Jerusalem. Of the many horrible images and symbols there, the one that stands out in my mind is a sculpture at the entrance to The Memorial for the Jewish Children. Several rectangular stone beams of differing height stand in a row perpendicular to the ground. Although the surfaces are smooth, the tops are broken and jagged. The contrasting textures illustrate the abrupt and cruel way in which so many young Jewish people were murdered.

It is always hard to accept the death of a young person—especially when life ends violently. In our culture we idolize youthfulness. Children and young adults are supposed to be immune from the pain and pressures of life. A person's death at a young age shatters our dreams for the person's future and threatens our own sense of invulnerability. If life stopped so suddenly for someone so young, what is in store for me?

Reading and commenting on James 4:14 during a funeral for a young person is helpful. "You do not know what your life will be like tomorrow. You are just a vapor that appears for a little while and then vanishes away." Like steam rising from a cup of coffee, life on Earth is short. At one moment it is here, and the next it is gone. A life, whatever its length in human terms, is of great value to God. As with that vanishing vapor, what is seen is real and cannot be denied, yet the length for which it can be observed has no bearing on its reality or value. The brevity of life ought to cause us to value the time and relationships we share on Earth. More important, we should be preparing for a life after this one is finished—a life that does not vanish but lasts forever.

Even someone who lives to be 100 has not been around very long. So why are we so troubled when someone dies? We want to live forever because the Lord put the concept of eternity in our hearts (Eccles. 3:11). It is natural to want to live as long as we can. However, few want to find eternal life God's way. We can share with others how to find the spiritual life that does not end when physical life is cut short.

Stillborn Children

Everyone born in our country is welcomed to the world with a birth certificate, and everyone who departs this life is granted a death certificate. The exception to the death certificate rule is applied to those who die before birth. In the state of Washington, fetal death certificates are issued for stillborn children only after they have lived more than twenty weeks in the womb. Apparently, the state of Washington has decided that human life begins in the twenty-first week of gestation.

It is legal in Washington to abort an unborn child even at full term. This raises several difficult questions. Should fetal death certificates be issued when a child dies at the hand of an abortionist beyond the twentieth week of pregnancy? Because the state recognizes a twenty-week-old fetus as a human being, should murder charges be pressed when a child of that age or older is killed by a physician? What is the government implying about human life in its fetal death certificate policies? Does the state accurately reflect God's view of life in the womb?

The Bible clearly affirms that the baby living and growing inside its mother—from the moment of conception—is a human being. When David wrote in Psalm 51:5 that in sin he was conceived, he was not referring to a wrong act that caused his mother to become pregnant. Instead, he was affirming that sin was present within him from the moment of conception.

The body is not sinful in itself, but is an instrument of sin (Rom. 1:24–32). David confirmed that from the beginning sin was present in his soul. It is the soul that marks mankind as unique among God's creation (Gen. 2:7).

The Bible asserts that human life begins at conception. Even before that moment, however, God knows each of us and has a plan for us. The Lord told Jeremiah, "Before I formed you in the womb I knew you, and before you were born I consecrated you" (Jer. 1:5).

Even the world acknowledges that the life inside a human mother is a human being. The World Medical Association's *Geneva Declaration,* which updates the Hippocratic oath, contains this line: "I will maintain the utmost respect for human life from the time of conception."

Any life, no matter how short, can be remembered and honored with a funeral. Services for stillborn children provide wonderful opportunities to teach the truth about the sanctity of human life.

Infants

The death of a child is the most painful and stress-filled experience a parent can endure. My greatest fear and worst nightmare is losing one of my children. I do not know how, apart from the grace of God, a parent can live through a child's death. When that kind of tragedy happens, we are called on to offer special strength, guidance, and support. Thinking through some of the issues surrounding the death of a child equips you to provide a more helpful service.

Why Do Young Children Die?

The first child for whom I performed a funeral was a victim of sudden infant death syndrome. She died while being cared for by a baby-sitter. The parents and the sitter suffered terribly after the death. The caregiver felt guilty for not keeping a closer eye on the girl (although nothing could have been done to prevent the death), and the parents felt guilty for having to leave their daughter with a sitter so they could work.

The question of why a child dies cannot be answered this side of heaven. You and I are not able to tap far enough into the sovereign mind and will of God to satisfy the concern. Some people suspect they are being punished for not being good parents, or that God is getting even with them for some sin. Even if the multitude of questions could be answered, I am not sure how comforting the truth would be to grieving parents.

Is My Child in Heaven?

In most cases (especially when the child was very young), I answer this question affirmatively. I realize there are differences of opinion on this matter, and the issue becomes complicated when variables such as the age of accountability and the doctrine of election are entered into the equation. I find some answers to this difficult problem in 2 Samuel 12, where the death of David's infant son is recorded. The reason for that death is clearly stated. The prophet Nathan warned, "Because by this deed [adultery and murder] you have given occasion to the enemies of the LORD to blaspheme, the child also that is born to you shall surely die" (2 Sam. 12:14). God took David's child as an act of discipline.

It would be dangerous and presumptuous to make the same conclusion today about the reason little ones die. While the king's son was suffering, David fasted and mourned. When his son died a week later, David washed and anointed himself, changed his clothes, worshiped, and ate a meal. Explaining his sudden change of behavior, he told his servants, "While the child was still alive, I fasted and wept; for I said, 'Who knows, the LORD may be gracious to me, that the child may live.' But now he has died; why should I fast? Can I bring him back again? I shall go to him, but he will not return to me" (2 Sam. 12:22–23).

Although some say David was simply referring to the fact that he himself would someday die, I disagree. What comfort is there in knowing that a grieving parent, too, will die? How does the acknowledgment of one's own mortality snap an agonizing mother out of her miserable condition? David knew he would see his son again. That brought him comfort. David knew that his son was going to spend eternity with the Lord and with him. That helped. The same relief can be experienced by parents of young children today when you communicate hope found in the Word of God.

Children and Young Adults

If the child is older (I have found no specific age in which to make a distinction between younger and older), I tell the parents that the Lord gives every person before he dies an opportunity to say yes or no to God about heaven. I explain that God has revealed himself to the world through his creation (Ps. 19:1–6; Rom. 1:20), through conscience (Rom. 2:14–16), the Bible (1 Thess. 2:13), and Jesus Christ (John 1:1–3, 14; 17:3; Heb. 1:1–2). I believe a child becomes accountable to God when he realizes God has made himself known to that child in one or more of the ways listed above.

I gently explain to grieving parents that while nothing can be done now about where their child will spend eternity, it is not too late for them to respond to the Lord who wants to reveal himself to them through Jesus Christ. But be careful not to be exploitive in an emotional situation. These hurting people may be asking the Lord to bring back their child or take away their pain, rather than seeking forgiveness through repentance.

Suicide

Nearly thirty thousand people in America take their own lives each year. Self murder is the third-highest cause of death among Americans between ages fifteen and twenty-four. The odds are that even if you perform only a handful of funerals, one will be for a person who has committed suicide.

I received a piece of mail from a Bible college I used to attend that stated a staff member "chose to go home to be with the Lord." The apostle Paul wrote that while being with Jesus is always preferable (2 Cor. 5:6–8), it is better to remain alive and please the Lord (v. 9). We may have the capacity to take our own lives, but I do not believe we have the right to take them. Life is a gift from God and is sacred. Abortion, suicide, and assisted suicide are becoming routine means of death. The church needs to be aware of and be vocal about what the Creator of life says concerning the sanctity of life. However, a funeral is not the time to expose the evils of abortion and suicide. The Sanctity of Life Sunday is at least one time a year that teachers and preachers can inform and equip the church to take a stand against these kinds of killings.

People often want to know if God is going to impose a more severe punishment on those who take their own lives. I have heard people say suicide is the unpardonable sin written of in 1 Corinthians 3:17: "If any man destroys the temple of God, God will destroy him, for the temple of God is holy, and that is what you are." But punishment for suicide is not an accurate interpretation of what Paul wrote—and for three reasons. First, *destroy* means "to corrupt or deprave," not "to kill or murder." Second Corinthians 11:3 and 1 Corinthians 15:33 use the same word in the sense of leading people astray and corrupting good morals. Second, the temple is a reference to the church as a whole, not an individual. Finally, the word you is plural, not singular. So while some believe the verse means, "If you kill yourself you are going to hell, even if you are a Christian," the words could accurately be translated, "If anyone leads the church of God astray, God will punish him, for the church of God is holy, and that is what all of you are." Eternal destiny is not determined by the means of death but by choices made about Jesus Christ before death. I believe suicide does not prevent a person from going to heaven.

When you perform a funeral for someone who committed suicide, should you mention that the person took his or her own life? This is a tough question to answer. People who attend usually know how the person died. If you mention the manner of death (you may want to ask the family for freedom to do that), you may give others permission to talk about suicide and work through complicated issues of grief more favorably. However, there is a strong enough stigma about suicide that you may not feel comfortable in talking about it openly at a funeral.

The most recent funeral I led for a person who committed suicide was for a man who had begun to lose his eyesight. To keep from having to adjust to that loss, he stepped into his back yard and put a bullet through his head. His wife heard the shot and ran out to find her husband still conscious. She cradled him in her arms until a helicopter airlifted him to a nearby trauma center, where he was pronounced dead on arrival. The family did not want me to mention how he died, but everyone knew. In fact, those who chose to view the body could see the exit wound on the side of his head, in spite of the funeral staff's efforts to conceal it.

Gunshot wounds are not the only way people take their lives. Jack Kevorkian has popularized physician-assisted suicide. A supreme court judge in Washington state recently overturned the will of the people expressed in a ballot initiative. He ruled that preventing a person from seeking physician-assisted suicide is unconstitutional. Regardless of that ruling, any means of suicide, legal or not, is wrong.

I believe it is not always a good idea to mention suicide when it was the cause of death. My first funeral involving suicide was for a middle-aged lady whose teenage son found her dead in the family den. The scene was so shocking and painful that the rest of the family was in strong denial for quite some time. Family members refused to consider suicide as an option for her cause of death. They tried hard to convince themselves that she died of natural causes. For me to talk about her death as suicidal would have been untimely and cruel.

On the other hand, if a family gives you permission to mention suicide, your talking about it may help others do the same. It also may bring into stark reality the pain and awkwardness of the act, and those who wrestle with suicidal tendencies might reconsider the idea when they see and hear the pain of others caused by those who succumbed to the temptation.

AIDS

If you have not yet conducted a funeral for someone who has died from complications of AIDS, you will. Statistics relating to AIDS are as alarming as they are controversial. While some people see AIDS and other kinds of sexually transmitted diseases as a part of God's judgment on sexual promiscuity (Rom. 1:18–32), remember that AIDS is not passed on only through homosexual contact.

For those who may have contracted AIDS innocently (such as through blood transfusions), questions of justice, sovereignty, and fairness will be asked. You need to be ready to offer God's solutions to those kinds of problems. Sin affects all of creation (Gen. 3:17–19; Rom. 5:12; 8:18–22), not just the one who sinned. It never seems right for an innocent person to suffer. We all have seen images of war-torn villages or famine-stricken communities where children die a slow, painful death. Questions about suffering have plagued the mind of man since sin entered the garden. Not until Jesus returns to establish his kingdom on Earth will people know no suffering. Pain is a fact of life, and in this life we cannot escape it. How much sweeter heaven will be for those who lived a life of suffering here.

Dying, death, and funerals provide wonderful opportunities to help people focus on the blessings of spending eternity with Jesus. A pastor friend of mine died after contracting AIDS through heterosexual and homosexual immoralities. As is typical with those who are dying with this disease, his physical decline lasted several months. However, he turned away from his sin, was forgiven by the Lord, and used his moral failure and spiritual recovery as an effective means of ministry. When he spoke to churches and other groups about the danger of sin and the importance of living for the Lord Jesus, he illustrated a message of forgiveness, joy, and hope with his own life.

Some who are dying with AIDS (or by any other slow means), often talk about what they want to be said at their funeral service. As best you can, honor those desires. The only requests I will not grant are those that condone immoral practices (such as homosexuality, fornication, adultery, drug abuse). I will not communicate "I love you" on behalf of the deceased to an immoral sex partner, or tell the audience that someone who lived in sin experienced a happy and meaningful life.

Murder

Does God have anything to say to teenage boys whose mother was murdered? One of my first funerals fit that scenario. Although the following Scripture does not specifically relate to the details of that death, it brought great comfort to the family.

> My soul, wait in silence for God only,
> For my hope is from Him.
> He only is my rock and my salvation,
> My stronghold; I shall not be shaken.
> On God my salvation and my glory rest;
> The rock of my strength, my refuge is in God.
> Trust in Him at all times, O people;
> Pour out your heart before Him;
> God is a refuge for us.
>
> Psalm 62:5–8

Murder destroys dreams and shatters families. It is good to know that God is a refuge. In him, and him alone, we can find the kind of stability that provides an even keel amid the most disastrous storms of life.

When someone is murdered, especially when the violence is random, the most painful and difficult question to answer is, Why? We know God is in control, but we sometimes cannot figure out why he allows evil and pain to be present. We know sin is at the root of all evil, but not too many families are going to be satisfied with that kind of theological response. Rather than trying to tell people why, let's focus on Who. Let's tell them that God is our refuge, our rock, our salvation, our stronghold, and our comforter. Let's tell them that in him hope is found. Perhaps we should remind them that God's Son was murdered. When hurting people pour their hearts out to him, and give him their pain and grief, he can replace sorrow with joy (Ps. 126:5).

Wicked People

How do you bury a bad guy? The old black and white cowboy movies give us the answer. Even though the stranger from out of town stole some horses and shot the sheriff before he was hung, he was given at least a decent burial before the show ended.

That attitude ought to be ours, too. No matter how rotten a person is, every human being deserves a polite farewell. Even if no one can come up with anything good to say during the eulogy, a funeral still can be held in honor of the deceased.

David eulogized Saul and Jonathan when Israel's first king and his son died in battle. Rather than taking advantage of a prime opportunity to blast the one who on several occasions had tried to kill him, David chose to bless the Lord's anointed. You can read David's eulogy, expressed as a dirge, in 2 Samuel 1:17–27. Nobody wants to hear how wicked the bad guy was, or to have you ask, "Aren't you glad he's gone?" Do you remember Thumper's advice in Walt Disney's film *Bambi?* "If you can't say somethin' nice, don't say nothin' at all."

When President Bill Clinton eulogized Richard Nixon, he mentioned that his last phone conversation with the former president and recent correspondence convinced him that Richard Nixon's spirit was very much alive to the end. I wonder what President Clinton meant by those words. Was he referring to recent "spirited" disagreements? Perhaps. If so, President Clinton illustrated that even negative things can be made to sound positive during a funeral. Because every human life is sacred and each of us is made in the image of God (Gen. 1:26–27), we ought to show basic respect for life by providing each person a decent and respectful burial.

CHAPTER 8

CARING FOR THE BEREAVED AFTER THE FUNERAL

*P*astors are quick to be present when an illness or accident threatens someone's life. Hospital and in-home visits, prayers, notes, and phone calls are routine expressions of support and encouragement. If death comes, the process of ministering to a bereaved family begins. Yet, one of the most important and often neglected aspects of death-related ministries is follow-up. Once the flurry of having to quickly prepare for and perform the service is over, how can you meaningfully care for the family? Getting through a funeral is relatively easy compared to enduring the backwash of grief that later overtakes the bereaved. The real work of mourning occurs months and years after a loved one is laid to rest.

I believe more ministers are not involved in funeral follow-up because helping others adjust to significant loss takes time. A common concern among pastors is the inability to do all that is expected of us. I sometimes feel like a circus performer spinning plates on top of those long flexible poles. The more

I serve the less time I seem to have to serve. When overloaded with pressures and expectations, it's easy to neglect important duties like funeral follow-up. Every time a ministry plate crashes at my feet I become a little bit more convinced that ministry would be much easier if it were not for people.

Many people, including pastors who have lost loved ones, are unfamiliar with the nature of bereavement, the process of grieving, and the purpose of mourning. Because we cannot fully understand or control these experiences, those of us who like to take charge of things can begin to feel out of place when trying to help others work through these things. Understanding the dynamics of bereavement can help us become better helpers to those who are in the grip of the powerful forces of grief and mourning.

Before we explore how to help those who continue to hurt after a loss, a few terms need to be defined. I am indebted to Dr. Alan Wolfelt and his excellent resource *Death and Grief: A Guide for Clergy* for clarifying the following terms.

Bereavement is a state caused by loss, such as death. Numerous types of losses can bring about a state of bereavement.

Grief is an emotional suffering caused by death or another form of bereavement. Grief involves a sequence of thoughts and feelings that follow the loss and accompany mourning. Grief is a process and as a result, is not a specific emotion like fear or sadness, but indeed is a constellation of a variety of thoughts, feelings, and behaviors. Grief is the internal meaning given to the external event.

Mourning is the outward expression of grief and bereavement. The specific ways in which people mourn are influenced by the customs of their culture. The mourning behavior exhibited may or may not be in agreement with true feelings of the bereaved; however, they may incur disapproval if they do not follow the prescribed social customs. Another way of defining mourning is to state that it is "grief gone public" or "showing one's grief outside of oneself."

The Nature of Bereavement

Bereave means "to deprive of something." Our English word is derived from an Anglo-Saxon root which means "to rob." Anyone who has lost a family member or close friend to death knows how it feels to be robbed of someone special. Regardless of one's emotions or thoughts, it is important to remember that God does not steal from us when someone dies, although that is how many feel. God is aware of and ultimately controls all things, even the time and way in which people die. "There is an *appointed* time for everything. And there is a time for every event under heaven—A time to give birth, and a time to *die*" (Eccles. 3:1–2, italics added).

Knowing that our days are limited (Ps. 90:10, 12) does not insulate us from struggling with the emotional and relational adjustments forced upon us when someone special dies. It takes time to get used to the fact that the person who used to be present will no longer be seen or heard. When someone who gave love, support, and encouragement is gone, people who benefited from those reinforcements will suffer an acute sense of loss.

The Purposes of Mourning

Too many people think that admitting or showing pain in the midst of loss is a sign of weakness. Hiding sorrow is a disabling cultural expectation we put on others. God gave us emotions and tear glands to be used.

Mourning Is a Natural Expression of Sorrow

Crying is a natural way to release tension and turmoil. In some cultures, outward expressions of sorrow are quite acceptable. In many cases private and public mourning are expected. My wife bought a replica of an ancient tear bottle while in Israel. Tear bottles were used to collect a mourner's expressions of grief. The bereaved could display the liquid they collected in the tiny vessel as a private demonstration of sorrow. It was a good thing for a wife's tear bottle to be full when her husband returned from war. After David was captured by the Philistines he wrote Psalm 56. Verse 8 says, "Put my tears in Thy bottle; are they not in Thy book?" God's chosen people have experienced suffering and heartache for millennia. We would do well to learn from their openness to sorrow by allowing others to mourn alone and in our presence.

Mourning Signals the Depth and Strength of Love

Isaiah told us the Messiah would be a man of sorrows, acquainted with grief (Isa. 53:3). The prophet was right. Jesus suffered emotional pain while he was among us, and he was not afraid to wear his emotions (positive and negative) on his sleeve. Our Lord sighed (literally groaned or grieved) when he healed the deaf man from the Decapolis region (Mark 7:34). Jesus wept over Jerusalem upon his final approach to that city from Galilee. On the night he was betrayed in the Garden of Gethsemane he said, "My soul is deeply grieved, to the point of death" (Matt. 26:38).

Outward expressions of sorrow are not signs of weakness but of strength. Jesus appeared untroubled by the news that his friend Lazarus was sick and dying (John 11). Not until Jesus was with the sisters of Lazarus four days after the man's death did Jesus express his love for Lazarus with tears. "Therefore, when Mary came where Jesus was, she saw Him, and fell at His feet, saying to Him, 'Lord, if You had been here, my brother would not have died.' When Jesus therefore saw her weeping, and the Jews who came with her, also weeping, He was deeply moved in spirit, and was troubled, and said, 'Where have you laid him?' They said to Him, 'Lord, come and see.' Jesus wept. And so the Jews were saying, 'Behold how He loved him!'" (John 11:32–36).

Do you see how the Jews interpreted Jesus' tears? "Behold how He loved him!" I sometimes wonder what the Jews would have thought if Jesus had remained stoic and dry-eyed. Our Lord experienced a full range of emotion in connection with the death of Lazarus. John 11:33 and 38 tell us Jesus was deeply moved in spirit and deeply moved within. Both verses use the same Greek word (translated "deeply moved") which means to snort in anger.

John 11:33 also mentions that Jesus was troubled, or disturbed, when he saw the way Mary was mourning. Our Lord may have been upset at the consequences of sin (death and sorrow) or the people's lack of faith in what he could do about those consequences (John 11:40). Regardless, he displayed a broad spectrum of emotion because of death. Are we any more spiritual than Jesus if we clam up and try to squelch our inner feelings when a loved one dies? Are we any less spiritual than the Son of God if we cry and mourn over loved ones we have lost? Even anger can be an appropriate grief response, if the emotion is expressed in healthy ways.

Mourning Moves Us toward Healing

Kathy Olsen wrote an interesting article for *Discipleship Journal* in 1981 about the cup of suffering Jesus mentioned in the Garden of Gethsemane. She makes a good point that a cup can only hold so much, and once the bearer drinks the contents, the vessel remains empty.

If we push the mourner (or he pushes himself) into premature abandonment of his sorrow . . . he may retain a residue of bitterness. It is as if we keep taking the cup of sorrow—a limited amount that must be drunk—out of his hands, saying, "No, you don't want to drink all this. Don't be sorrowful, because you know God is sovereign and will work this for good. You can be happy now because of those promises if you exercise faith." So the mourner forgets the half-drunk cup of sorrow still sitting in his soul, and it ferments and grows bacteria and spawns a root of bitterness that springs up and bears poisonous fruit.

When we allow mourners to drink the cup of suffering that comes with loss, healing arrives much sooner. That means we must let people mourn the way they need to, as long as their expressions of grief are healthy. In time, their mourning will cease.

Tracing the word mourn or mourning in the Bible with a concordance reveals that the time of one's sorrow can end. We find phrases like "the time of mourning was ended," "the days of mourning for him were past," and "then the days of weeping and mourning for Moses came to an end." Ecclesiastes 3:4 reminds us there is "a time to weep, and a time to laugh; a time to mourn, and a time to dance." Our Lord assured us that those who mourn will someday be comforted (Matt. 5:4). Comfort cannot come without pain first having been present.

These principles and promises of Scripture should not be used to persuade a person to hurry up and get over sorrow. Instead, we need to assure those who mourn that God and we will help them, in time, to get through their grief. "Weeping may last for the night, but a shout of joy comes in the morning" (Ps. 30:5).

Many styles of mourning can be found in the Scriptures. People cried and wailed. They wore sackcloth and ashes. Some fasted and prayed. Others tore their clothes or cut their hair.

There is a strong connection between appropriate demonstrations of grief and healing. Some people, however, in their desire to do something with their pain, act inappropriately. We should intervene when mourners indulge in alcohol or excessive eating. I know of some who have gone on spending sprees or sexual binges. Too often mourners will plunge into anything that does not feel like grief. These are unhealthy grief reactions.

A friend who is an audio technician told me about another technician who was asked by a woman to place a radio transmitter in her husband's casket. She made this strange request so she could hear her husband call out to her if he should come back to life.

A better thing we can do for the bereaved is help them fully embrace and live through their grief. This may be why other cultures hire professional mourners—to encourage others to act out their feelings of loss and sorrow. Hired mourners function like worship leaders in a church or cheerleaders at a football game. They encourage us to do what we need to do for the benefit of ourselves and others. Public mourning not only honors the dead but bonds the brokenhearted, keeping the bereaved from feeling alone in their sorrow.

Solomon advised us it is better to feel our sadness at a time of loss than to indulge ourselves in pleasure. "It is better to go to a house of mourning than to go to a house of feasting, because that is the end of every man, and the living takes it to heart. Sorrow is better than laughter, for when a face is sad a heart may be happy. The mind of the wise is in the house of mourning, while the mind of fools is in the house of pleasure" (Eccles. 7:2–4).

Individuals who do not responsibly acknowledge, work out, and live through their emotions could be headed for deeper problems. Edgar Jackson reveals in *Resources for Ministry in Death and Dying* that some physical illnesses result from psychological stress caused by grief. Research shows that admissions to hospitals are higher among the grief stricken than among the general population. People who do not handle their grief in a healthy fashion end up having their body do the work of grief for them in unhealthy ways.

The Process of Grief

Elisabeth Kübler-Ross popularized five stages of grief (denial, anger, bargaining, depression, and acceptance) in her book *On Death and Dying.* Other researchers have noted that grief can be more complicated and broader than the Kübler-Ross map. There are pluses and minuses to familiarizing oneself with any model of grief. On the positive side, grief research helps those who are hurting anticipate healing. The dangers of relying on any systemized pattern of suffering is that those who are grieving may try to push themselves to the next step to facilitate an unnaturally fast rate of healing. Rushing the process sometimes brings pseudohealing.

We likely could find as many models of grief work as there are grief researchers. For this reason I prefer not to tell a mourner what next to expect in his sorrow. Instead, I try to encourage the one who has experienced a significant loss that each painful period, as real as it is, will pass. Caring for those who are grieving is a delicate art, but it is not as complicated or awkward as many fear. The simple gift of our presence is perhaps the greatest support we can offer to those who hurt.

I was mowing the lawn when my recently widowed neighbor pulled into her driveway. I shut off the lawnmower and walked over to her house to offer comfort. We chatted about the long-awaited sunshine and the flowers that were beginning to bloom. Then I asked, "How are you doing?" She knew I was asking about the adjustment to losing her husband of thirty-four years. We had talked about his death and her reactions before. In the hospital while her husband was lying in a coma we talked and prayed together. In her home before and after the funeral we talked about his life and his death. The brief conversation that sunny Saturday afternoon was an extension of care I had been giving all along. Her response was typical. "Oh, fine. It's hard, but I'm okay."

I knew she could cope with her loss. She is a Christian and has good support from her church and many friends. Yet, I wanted to let her know that I genuinely cared. I didn't know if anyone was talking with her beyond the easy surface issues. So I asked her again, "How are you really doing, Lois? Are things around the house being taken care of? Are you eating all right? Would you like to have a cup of coffee and talk for a while about your feelings and how you are handling your grief?"

"No thanks, Dan," she said. "Not today. There are times when I cry a lot and there are times when I am doing very well. Today is a good day. I have been asking God to make himself real to me while I adjust. He did that when you came over to talk with me."

I tried not to show it, but her words floored me. God made himself real to this woman through a brief conversation. I thought to myself, "Is that all it takes to make God real to people—a simple conversation?"

Practical Suggestions for Follow-Up

That experience with Lois reminded me of the story of the little boy who was frightened by a thunderstorm. He called out to his father, "Daddy, come here. I'm scared."

"Son," the father replied, "God loves you and he will take care of you."

"I know God loves me. But right now I need somebody who has skin on."

As long as we "wear skin" we can show mourners who God is and what he is like. Here are some practical things we can do:

- Make brief visits to the home. Share your memories of the deceased. Look through photo albums. Be ready to help those who are grieving talk through plans that cannot be realized because of the death.

- Make brief phone calls. Try to do this at least one week and one month after the death. Pray over the phone if appropriate.
- Send short notes with a Scripture promise. These expressions of encouragement will be especially appreciated around holidays, wedding anniversaries, birthdays, and the anniversary of the death.
- Visit the gravesite with the family. Offer to be present when the headstone is placed.
- Invite the bereaved to church if they do not have a church family. Be willing to accept the fact that your ministry may not be suited for everyone. Those you care for at the time of death may find another church more appropriate for their worship needs.
- Be ready to offer referrals for specialized counseling. Funeral homes can assist you with referrals to Survivors of Suicide, Parents of Murdered Children, SHARE (support for parents and siblings whose infant family member has died), Widowed Persons Service/American Association of Retired Persons, and other agencies and organizations specializing in help for the bereaved.
- Equip a group of people in your church to support your funeral follow-up ministry. Just because you performed a funeral does not mean you are the only one who can help a bereaved person.

EPILOGUE

*I*n the introduction to this book you met Barbara, whose college-age daughter was killed in an automobile accident. I'm happy to say the skills I've written about enabled me to minister significantly to her and her family. Barbara was able to talk openly with me about her loss and I was able to talk freely with her about the Lord Jesus.

I met with family members after the funeral for some follow-up. They invited me back into their home because in preparing for and performing the funeral I had shown them I cared about the way their family was being changed. We talked about how difficult it would be to adjust to life without Barbara's daughter. I told them about the people from our church who were praying for them and assured them that God promises to heal the brokenhearted.

During our conversation I learned that Barbara's husband was a Christian. In that meeting Barbara gave her life to the Lord. Her husband made the decision to refocus his life on Christ. They now attend their own church, and over the years he has become a deacon.

Not all families you work with will emerge from their loss with this kind of healing and recovery. However, more will, if you can skillfully and compassionately lead them toward Christ. The principles in this book, if developed and applied, will help you do that. It is my prayer that God will give to you as rich and meaningful a funeral ministry as he has given me. Not only have I learned to love people more deeply, but I am longing to experience what so many believers have gone on to enjoy—being in the presence of our Lord Jesus in heaven. See you there!

$\mathcal{F}$UNERAL INTERVIEW FORM

Personal Information

Name of deceased _____

Date of birth _____

Date of death _____

Cause of death _____

Spouse _____

Anniversary _____

Funeral home _____

Phone _____

Date of service _____

Type of service _____

Contact person _____

Phone _____

Relationship _____

Interview Checklist

Work/Career

Personality/Lifestyle

Beliefs/Spiritual background

Information about the death

How to be remembered/Final comment

Service components (music/speakers/poems/Scripture)

ℱUNERAL CHECKLIST

❑ **Preparation**
- ❑ Notification from funeral home. Start a file card for the deceased. Verify and record:
    - ❑ Name of deceased.
    - ❑ Name, address, and phone number of family contact person.
    - ❑ Date, place, and time of service. Check personal schedule for conflicts, and enter funeral information on personal calendar.
    - ❑ Kind of service (if already decided).
    - ❑ Means of death.
- ❑ Contact prayer team and describe prayer requests.
- ❑ Arrange appointment to visit with family for funeral preparations.
    - ❑ Call family contact person.
    - ❑ Schedule a planning meeting with family.
    - ❑ Determine location for meeting, and secure driving instructions.
    - ❑ Record family planning meeting in personal calendar.
- ❑ Meet with family for funeral planning.
    - ❑ Introduce self.
    - ❑ Record names of family members on notepad.
    - ❑ Interview family about deceased.

❑ Verify name, spelling, and pronunciation.

❑ Personal information (marriage, children, date of birth and death).

❑ Work/career.

❑ Personality/lifestyle.

❑ Hobbies/special interests/volunteer activities.

❑ Beliefs/spiritual background.

❑ Information about the death.

❑ How the deceased wanted to be remembered.

❑ Final comment from deceased to those at the service.

❑ Verify date, place, and time of service.

❑ Verify type of service (graveside, memorial, funeral).

❑ Determine components of service.

   ❑ Music (taped, instrumental, vocal).

   ❑ Speakers/involvement from others.

   ❑ Readings (poems, Scripture).

❑ Review order of service.

❑ Ask for questions.

❑ If appropriate, arrange to view the body with the family.

❑ Confirm when you will arrive at funeral home/cemetery.

❑ Pray.

❑ Leave business card.

❑ **Personal Preparations for the Service**

❑ Verify the consistency of information from funeral home and family.

❑ Thematically/chronologically sort information about the deceased.

❑ Prayerfully select passages of Scripture for the service.

❑ Outline/write comments to be made during the service.

❏ Outline the order of service (check spelling and grammar).

❏ Make copies of the order of service for funeral staff and service participants.

❏ **Final Preparations on the Day of the Service**

❏ Arrive at least thirty minutes before the service begins.

❏ Check in with the funeral director to receive clergy card/honorarium.

❏ Ask if there are any last-minute changes.

❏ Give copies of the order of service to the funeral director.

❏ Give a copy of the order of service to the organist or piano player and review the order of service together.

❏ Contact family members.

❏ Comfort them with your words.

❏ Ask if there is anything to be added to the service.

❏ View the body with the family, if appropriate.

❏ Pray with the family, if appropriate.

❏ Ask if there are any last-minute questions.

❏ Spend some quiet time in an office alone to pray over and review the service.

❏ **Perform the Service**

❏ Escort the casket if appropriate.

❏ Be seated during the musical prelude.

❏ Follow the outline of the service.

❏ If there is a viewing at the end of the service, stand near the head of the casket as people are led forward by the funeral staff.

❏ Visit with the family (at the casket) when guests have been dismissed.

- ❏ If the service will conclude at a cemetery:
  - ❏ Escort the casket to the funeral coach. Follow the funeral director's instructions.
  - ❏ Be seated in the front passenger seat of the coach when the casket is secured.
  - ❏ Escort the casket to the graveside.
  - ❏ Perform a brief graveside service when the funeral director gives the ready signal.
  - ❏ Visit with the family at the gravesite when the service is completed.
  - ❏ Offer to follow up with the family in the near future.

❏ **Follow-Up Suggestions**

- ❏ Ask the funeral director for feedback on how to make your next service more meaningful.
- ❏ Reflect on the quality of your leadership at the service. Make notes on how you can improve the next service you lead.
- ❏ Send a note of encouragement to the family two weeks after the service.
- ❏ Invite the family to church.
- ❏ Refer the family to a grief support group if one is available.
- ❏ Offer to be present with the family when the headstone is placed at the grave.
- ❏ Offer to visit the grave with the family.
- ❏ Visit with the family in the home.
- ❏ Call family contacts to let them know you have not forgotten them.
- ❏ Send a note to a widow/widower on the wedding anniversary.
- ❏ Send a note or card to the family on the date of the deceased's birth or death.
- ❏ Encourage a family in your church to "adopt" the grieving family.

$\mathscr{S}$AMPLE FUNERALS

While I follow brief outlines of the kinds of services I perform, no two funerals have ever been the same. Each funeral you lead should be as unique as the person you are honoring. For this reason, the sample formats that follow should serve only as examples. Multiple variables must be considered when putting together a service. It takes quality time to plan and lead a first-rate service.

The following samples are typical of the funerals I have conducted over the years. I wrote out my notes so you can get a feel for the services. It works best to read the Scripture passages at the points they are listed.

Graveside Service for a Christian

(*Circumstances:* This service was for my secretary's father, Herman Haug, who became a Christian on his deathbed. He died while I was traveling abroad and I could not conduct the memorial service for him. I led the following service later, when the family had his remains placed in a mausoleum.)

Read Psalm 90:1–2 and Psalm 91:1–2.

Herman Haug lived a long life. You have many memories of him. As you think about the years spent with him and the contributions all of you made to one another, there are many significant and precious highlights that come to mind. But the most significant event in the life of Herman Haug occurred in his final hours. He acknowledged his need for Jesus Christ. That decision was a long time in coming. You prayed for your husband, father, and father-in-law for many years. I know that he wrestled with what it means to embrace Christ. His decision was well-thought-out, and it was the best decision he could have made.

Because of that decision, Herman is now in heaven. We'll see him there when it is our time to go home. Allow me to read for you what the Bible says about heaven.

Read Revelation 21:1–5 and Revelation 22:1–5.

Herman would agree with everything I have read today, and he would want to add a whole lot more to our understanding of heaven. He lives there. He knows what heaven is like. He knows what Jesus looks like. He has actually seen Jesus' scars and the glorious angels who surround his Savior.

We are not home yet. We probably have several years left until we see Herman again and meet our Savior. Until then, we are establishing a place where we can remember Herman, anticipating the day we are finally reunited. It is at this place where you will return with mixed emotions. A place where you will laugh and cry. That's okay. It's not wrong to grieve, so long as we grieve with hope.

Read 1 Thessalonians 4:13–18.

God will re-create and form a new body for Herman Haug. When we are taken from this earth to be with Jesus, Herman and every other believer who lives in heaven will receive a brand new body. I want to conclude our service this morning with prayer. As I do, we will commit these ashes to the earth from which they came, knowing that God will reunite us with Herman, and together we will be with the Lord forever.

Prayer: Father, thank you for Herman Haug. Thank you that he made life's most important decision. Thank you that when he called out to you, you were there. Thank you that Herman is in heaven with you, and there he awaits our reunion. May we be found faithful to you until that day. We thank you that you gave Herman not only spiritual life, but physical life as well. Thank you for the family you gave him, and the memories they share together. And now that we are establishing a place of remembrance here, we commit these ashes to the earth. From earth we are created, and to the earth we must return. We joyfully anticipate that moment when our Savior calls us from this life to the next, when all the saints in Christ will be clothed with new bodies, and from that day forward we shall always be with the Lord. Come quickly, Lord Jesus. Amen.

Graveside Service for a Child

(*Circumstances:* This service was conducted for a three-month-old girl, Ashley, who died of sudden infant death syndrome. She was being cared for by a neighbor when she died. I was present when the coroner took the baby from the parents for an examination. The parents asked me to explain to her siblings that their sister would no longer be coming home. If my memory serves me correctly, Ashley's mother was a Christian when her daughter died, and her father became a Christian shortly after the funeral.)

Read poem written by a family friend.

Read obituary from clergy card.

Prayer: Lord, we do not understand everything you do, or the things you allow to happen. We do know that the Bible says you are in control of everything, however disappointing or displeasing the circumstances might be. The one request I have of you today is that you help this family find the strength in you they need. Encourage us today. Please strengthen us. Thank you for being here. May your presence here with us today make a difference in the way we face each new day. In Jesus' name, amen.

Read Isaiah 41:10; 43:2, 3a.

We have all come here to this place today with a lot of questions on our minds. The one demanding greatest attention is, Why? Why this family? Why Ashley? Why did she die so young? Why SIDS? Why did God allow this to happen? These are definitely important questions, but I do not think they can all be answered on this side of heaven. The answers I do have, I want to give to you. I want what I say to give hope and strength, for God has promised that he would give us those things in our times of need.

I can tell you today where Ashley is. I can tell you how to see her again, and I can tell you what our response now to Ashley's death should be. In order to do that, I must read to you a story from the Bible. It is a true account of another child who died at an early age. The child was a son born to David, the greatest human king Israel knew. Found in this story are answers to some of the questions we are asking.

Read 2 Samuel 12:15–23.

Although the events that occurred in this incident happened thousands of years ago, the details are recorded in the Bible for a reason. That reason is to give you and me hope and comfort today. This story tells us much, but I want to focus on three facts that I believe will be of comfort to you.

First, Ashley is at peace; she is not suffering. The Bible says in heaven there is no suffering, no pain, no tears. Your little one is in the presence of Jesus. Our Lord loved little children and is loving your child. And as much as I know you would rather be the ones to hold her now, there is no other place she would rather be right now than in heaven.

Second, I can say with confidence that your child is in heaven. Hell is for those who reject God. Ashley was too young to make a conscious choice to reject God. Your child was too young to commit a sin, and was, therefore, carried directly into the presence of God by her guardian angel. Your child wants to be with Jesus, and she wants you to be with him, too.

Finally, you can see your child again in heaven. I said a moment ago that your daughter was brought directly into heaven because she was not old enough to sin. What about us? We've been around for a while. Anybody with a brain can look around us and realize that none of what we see appeared simply by chance. The universe is too vast and the human body too complex for life to have evolved haphazardly. There is a creator, and we know it.

We have a moral obligation to the Creator to acknowledge him. We are responsible to the one who made us. The Bible says if we reject him, he will reject us (2 Tim. 2:12). But on the other hand, Jesus said if we believe in him, he will bring us to the Father in heaven when we die (Matt. 10:32).

Your child was too young to either believe in or reject God. It is my belief that God, in his grace, brought Ashley to heaven simply because of her young age. King David had the same confidence when he said, "I shall go to him, but he shall not come to me." Your child is in heaven because she was too young to make that choice on her own. But what about you? What have you done about your obligation to God? Have you rejected God, or do you believe in him?

When I say believe, I am talking about more than just acknowledging that God exists. Even the devil is convinced that

God exists. To believe in God means you acknowledge him on his terms. God's conditions are rather strict. Many people do not like them, but they are true and binding nonetheless.

Present the gospel.

Turn to Christ. And do not neglect turning to one another. I have seen the closeness in this family, and you need to remain close. Turn to one another for help, support, and encouragement. Don't allow yourselves not to grieve. Let it happen. Let God help you through one another.

Prayer: God, you promised you would be here for us when we are in trouble or have a need. We need you. Our hearts are filled with pain and sorrow, yet at the same time we know that you are in control. I admit to you that we have a hard time accepting what you have allowed to happen. Keep us from turning away from you when instead we should be turning to you. As we leave this place today, we say good-bye to Ashley. Her memory will forever live within our hearts. Although she was not here for very long, we are all the richer because of our brief acquaintance with her. For the few short months she was ours, we thank you. She is now yours. Amen.

Funeral for a Christian

(*Circumstances:* This service was for my friend, John, who was killed at work. I gave some details surrounding his death, and my response to it, at the beginning of chapter 7 on leading difficult funerals. This was a full funeral with the service beginning in the chapel and concluding at graveside.)

Chapel Service

Read 1 Thessalonians 4:13–18.

Pray on theme of comfort and hope.

Listen to taped song, "Memories."

Read obituary from clergy card.

Listen to taped song, "Those Who Sow with Tears Shall Reap with Joy."

Nobody in this room, one week ago, thought they would be here today. The death of John Magby was sudden and un-expected . . . at least from our perspective. John's accident was not an accident. From God's point of view it was, and is, a part of his plan for you and even for me.

I don't know or understand God's timing or what he wants to make of all of this. But I do know God and his perfect char-acter. Everything God does, and all that he allows to hap-pen, has a purpose. In the Bible, the prophet Isaiah wrote these words:

Read Isaiah 55:6–13.

Our hope rests in God alone, not in the circumstances of life—or for that matter, death.

John knew God. I remember the day John and JoLynn sur-rendered their lives to Jesus Christ. What a beautiful trans-formation occurred, and continues to occur. I saw not only this couple change, but extended family members as well, as they, too, received Jesus Christ as Lord and Savior.

John loves the Lord. He is with his Savior now. John was not afraid to share with others his relationship with his God. John was very excited and bold. I know he has talked with many of you. I know you saw changes that Jesus Christ made in his life. Those kinds of changes cannot be explained apart from knowing Christ yourself. Those same kinds of changes can be yours through Christ also.

Prior to knowing Christ, John admitted that he had a sense of emptiness in his life. He felt that something was missing, that something deep inside was unsettled. He enjoyed good friends, stable financial conditions, a loving family, and many satisfying memories of crunching opponents on the football field. It was not until he acknowledged a spiritual problem that John could have peace in his life. His spiritual problem was sin, a falling away or separation from God. When John understood that Jesus came to this earth to die for him, to pay the death penalty for sin on his behalf, John eagerly accepted Christ's gift of forgiveness.

It was at the grave of a close friend that Jesus said, "I am the resurrection and the life. He who believes in me, though he should die, shall live." John believed in Jesus and received him as his Savior. Today, John is alive in heaven with his Savior, Jesus Christ. Jesus is the only way to find peace in life, like John found, and to have eternal life in heaven after death, like John is experiencing now.

John not only knew God, he knew the Bible as well. Yesterday, I spent some time reviewing the many notes he wrote in the margin and back of his Bible. He had a favorite verse. Philippians 1:6 says, "For I am confident of this very thing, that He who began a good work in you will perfect it until the day of Christ Jesus." The good work that God started in John's life is not over yet. God will continue to use the influence of John Magby until Jesus Christ returns.

When Jesus comes, John wants you to be ready to go back to heaven with the Lord. You can be ready to go to heaven by receiving Jesus Christ as your Savior. That is done by saying, "Lord Jesus, I know that I need you. I need you to take away my sin, to give me forgiveness and peace, and to take me home to heaven when I die. Thank you for dying on the cross for my sins. Thank you for rising from the dead so I can be forgiven. Thank you for becoming my Savior, because I truly believe in you."

John would want you to make a commitment to Jesus Christ if you have never done that before. I know that's what

John would want, because I know he has experienced something that none of us has experienced—life after death. John is with Jesus and they are both asking the Father to bring you into the family of God by believing in Jesus.

Come to Christ today. Not for John, or the family, but for you. That is all John would want from you as you are here to honor him today.

Closing prayer

Graveside Conclusion

Read 1 Corinthians 15:51–58.

Jesus wept at the graveside of his close friend Lazarus. He knew the pain, shock, confusion, and grief that death brings. More than that, he knew what death is like. Jesus Christ also died, but rose again. That's what Easter is all about. Because Jesus was victorious over death, he offers that same victory to those who believe in him.

Because Jesus once stood in the kind of place in which we now stand, we can turn to him for strength and hope. Jesus said, "Come unto me all you who are weary and heavy laden, and I will give you rest."

You can also turn to one another. God uses people to function as his hands, arms, and heart of compassion when we need a physical touch or hug. I thank God for the closeness of John's family. Continue talking and laughing about your memories of John. There will be many emotions you face in the weeks and months ahead. You will feel things you never thought you would feel. You will think things you never imagined you would think. When you are angry and confused and are not sure that you are going to make it through another day, you need to know that the emotions running wild through you are normal responses to this kind of loss.

Someday we will see John again (and your mother, too, JoLynn). What a great day that will be. Death for a Christian is a graduation. John beat us to the punch. We'll see him soon.

Prayer: Father, we thank you for John Magby. We thank you for what he has meant to us in the past, what he means to us now, and what he will mean to us for the rest of our lives. A part of us does not want to leave this place today, because it means saying good-bye. We are comforted in knowing that even though John is gone, you are here. You are always with us, no matter where we are. You have promised to never leave us.

We need to leave this place. We need to say good-bye to John. As we do, Lord, we commit the body of John Magby back to the earth from which it came. We know that when your Son returns from heaven, you will give to John and to each of us a new body, a perfect one that will never again die. Then, we shall forever be together with the Lord. Come quickly, Lord Jesus. Amen.

Funeral for a Non-Christian

(*Circumstances:* This was the first funeral I performed. It was for a forty-four-year-old woman who had committed suicide. A family member introduced the widowed husband to the Lord on the way to the cemetery after the chapel service.)

Chapel Service

Organ prelude

Opening remarks

We are here today to reflect on the life of and to honor Darlene. She was a woman whose life contributed to all of yours, and for that each one of us is grateful. We are here to express our grief for the death of a wife, a mother, a sister, and a loved one. She is a person who is loved by all of you and will be missed by all of you.

Read obituary from clergy card.

Read (with audience) Psalm 23 on memorial card.

Prayer for hope, comfort, encouragement

Soloist

We can never be fully prepared for the death of a loved one. Because this is true in our case, I realize there are heightened feelings of shock, helplessness, and perhaps even hopelessness. There are feelings of loss, disappointment, confusion, grief, darkness, and even guilt. I am sure that many of you have thought more than once, "Perhaps there is something we could have done to avoid this death." Our regrets cannot change what has happened. But what we can do is remember the past, learn to cope with the present, and anticipate a brighter future.

Many of you have fond memories of Darlene and the kind of person she was. She has been described to me as a caring, compassionate individual. When her children were sick, she would tend to them without complaint. She was a woman of compassion, and expressed her sympathy for many—from stray cats to stray people. Darlene had a reputation for helping those less fortunate than she was, even if they were strangers. More than once she fed those she did not know. She really cared.

To her husband and family, she was a teammate, a companion. Rarely did she work outside the home so she could be available to those who loved her most. Her family was her priority. Her relationship with her husband was described to me as one person in two bodies. She was a committed lady.

She was also practical—some would say frugal. She knew the value of a dollar and didn't squander a dime. She knew the difference between a need and a want, and she wanted only that which she really needed. She recognized beauty and respected it. She made things with her hands and enjoyed sewing, cooking, gardening, and various other kinds of crafts and projects.

In the midst of all these memories, there is much to enjoy and cherish. I encourage you to relive the times you shared with Darlene and talk about them together. Recalling these things means the memories you have of her are of value to you and that they are worthy of sharing. I believe Darlene would not want you to plague yourselves with an overabundance of questions, such as, "Why this death? Why this way?" Fill your minds instead with thanks for the good times you shared.

At present, there is sadness and grief. Those feelings always accompany a significant loss. Even Jesus wept when his friend died. It's okay to grieve. But don't grieve alone. You have others who are feeling and thinking the same things you are. Jesus knows how you feel. He said you can come to him with your burdens and he will carry them for you. He said in him we can find rest for our souls.

That rest does not have to be temporal, for this life alone. It can be eternal and last forever. True peace and rest are found in Jesus. Darlene would now affirm that if she could. She has already experienced something you and I know little about, and that is life after death. She knows that life exists beyond the grave. If she could, she would encourage you to prepare for the afterlife right now, because no one knows when the next funeral will be. No one knew last week that we would be here today for Darlene. Who's next? And when will that service be held? If the next one is for you next week, will you be ready to face eternity?

The way to prepare for eternity is to embrace Jesus Christ. The cross before us in this chapel is not just a religious symbol, it represents life that lasts forever—but only for those who believe.

Present the gospel.

Grief and sadness are normal, and should move us to consider the spiritual realities of life both now and forever. So what do we do about the future? Where do we go from here? In the immediate future, you can support the family. You can pray for them, visit them, talk with them, and cry with them. They need you, and you need them. Your lives will no longer be the same. Help each other adjust to a life without Darlene.

Ultimately, I would point you to God and his words in the Bible:

Read 1 Corinthians 15:51–52, 55, 57.

Jesus Christ overcame death by rising from the dead. With that, he paved the way for you and me to go to heaven. Through faith in him, you will get there some day. Let's think about that as we listen to another song sung for us.

Solo

Prayer of thanks for comfort and salvation offered through Christ

Graveside Conclusion

We are here to bring some closure to an event that has unalterably changed our lives. In these next few moments, we will be saying good-bye to Darlene, and then leave, preparing to adjust to a life without her. But in these moments, I want to encourage you by reading one more passage of Scripture. These few verses remind us that whatever circumstances challenge us, God can be with us through them all. The verses tell us of the strength of God's love and how the reality of his presence can bring comfort, strength, and hope.

Read Romans 8:35, 38–39.

The apostle Paul wrote in these verses that even death cannot separate us from God's love. His use of the word death is rather generic. While I believe the first thing he means is our own death, I also believe that its use can mean the death of anyone else.

I would feel very uncomfortable in saying that Darlene's death had anything to do with God's love or lack of love for you. In fact, these verses I just read give strong affirmation to the fact that God's love cannot be taken from us by any force, no matter how great. There are times when God's love may not seem real. There are times when we may feel very far from God. It is those times when we are told to draw near to God and he will draw near to you.

We draw near him through prayer, through reading the Bible, and by learning more about him through Christian friends and by going to church. I want you to know that God does love you. Darlene's death is not an expression of hatred or punishment. It may be a call to draw near to God and receive his love. It is there. It is available. And once you receive it, nothing can separate you from it.

As I mentioned in the chapel, faith in God means believing in Jesus and reaching out to him to make your relationship with him personal. If you look for and reach out for God, he will make himself known to you, because he is right here. All you have to do is open the door of your life, and invite him in. He wants to show you how much he loves you, but he cannot do that unless you let him.

As I pray in a moment, we will be saying good-bye to Darlene. We will be committing her body to the earth from which it came. I will also be praying a prayer that is an expression of faith, asking God to come into your life, that you open up to him. If that is your desire today, pray silently with me, and after the service tell me that you prayed with me.

Prayer: Father in heaven, we are here today because of a terrible tragedy. Help us have the faith to know that you can turn tragedy into triumph and give meaning to all that has happened in the last several days. No one who knew Darlene will ever be the same. Lives have been changed, and there is nothing we can do to change what has happened. However, we can change our orientation to those events by asking you to make your love real to us. Thank you for promising that nothing would separate us from your love—not even death.

As an expression of faith, to show you that I want your love, I am telling you now that I am a needy person. I need you in my life. I need your forgiveness so you can come into my life and change it. I know that the only way my life can change is by admitting why it is so imperfect and incomplete—why it sometimes lacks your love when I need it most. I believe that Jesus died on the cross to forgive my sins, and that he was buried and rose again from the dead. I now ask you to forgive my sins and come into my life and make me the kind of person you want me to be. Thank you for your forgiveness. Thank you for your love.

At this time, we commit Darlene's body to the earth. You said we are created from the earth and to the earth we must return. We now return the body of Darlene.

Give us your daily grace, God, to make it through these difficult times. I ask especially on behalf of the family, Darlene's husband and children, that your presence and love be felt in that home. Provide for them in ways only you can. In Jesus' name, amen.

$\mathscr{B}$IBLIOGRAPHY

Egan, Gerard. *The Skilled Helper.* Monterey, Calif.: Brooks/Cole Publishing Company, 1982.

Engle, Paul E., editor. *Baker's Funeral Handbook: Resources for Pastors.* Grand Rapids: Baker Books, 1996.

Gaither, Gloria, and Shirley Dobson. *Let's Make a Memory.* Waco: Word, 1983.

Kübler-Ross, Elisabeth. *On Death and Dying.* London: Macmillan, 1969.

Lawrenz, Mel, and Daniel Green. *Life after Grief: How to Survive Loss and Trauma.* Grand Rapids: Baker Books, 1995.

———. *Overcoming Grief and Trauma.* Grand Rapids: Baker Books, 1995.

Olsen, Kathy. "A Time To Mourn." *Discipleship Journal* 41 (1987).

Platt, Larry A., and Roger G. Branch. *Resources for Ministry in Death and Dying.* Nashville: Broadman Press, 1988.

Rogers, Fred. *Talking with Young Children about Death.* Pittsburgh: Family Communication, Inc., 1979.

Wolfelt, Alan D. *Death and Grief: A Guide for Clergy.* Muncie, Ind.: Accelerated Development, Inc., Publishers, 1988.

"World." *Time,* June 19, 1989, 38–39.

Daniel Scott Lloyd has served in pastoral ministries on the West Coast, currently in Federal Way, Washington. He has also served as an on-call minister for a funeral chapel and has conducted workshops for pastors on effective funeral ministry. His B.S. in Christian education and counseling comes from Biola University and his M.A. in marriage and family ministries from Talbot School of Theology.